Ripples of Generative AI

*How Generative AI Impacts, Informs, and Transforms
Our Lives*

Jacob Emerson

Table of Contents

1

Introduction

Imagine a world where devices can predict and produce what we desire, where artwork can be generated on the whim of a machine, and where virtual assistants don't just answer queries but anticipate our needs before we even articulate them. This is a glimpse into a future driven by a revolutionary technology known as Generative Artificial Intelligence.

In this book, we are on an exploratory journey through the complex world of Generative Artificial Intelligence. We will venture through its intricate mechanics, vivid applications, profound social impacts, and the vast horizons of its future potential. While this introduction offers a gentle first touch, the subsequent chapters will provide in-depth information about this topic.

Artificial Intelligence has been a buzzword for decades, sparking both wonder and fear in people's minds. There is a technology that has the potential to transform everything about the way we live, work, and interact. This technology is generative AI. But before we dive deep into its topic, let us start by understanding what Artificial Intelligence (AI) is.

Imagine you are in your kitchen preparing dinner. You have done this many times before, so you don't need to think about each step. You instinctively know when the onions are finely chopped, when the oven is hot enough, and when the steak is perfectly cooked. This is a form of intelligence, a human one, grounded in learning and experience. Now, suppose you could impart this intelligence to a machine, enabling it to learn from experience and make decisions based on that learning. This is what we refer to as artificial intelligence (AI).

AI is a vast, varied landscape, teeming with different branches and specialties. One such specialty is generative AI, which is similar to giving a machine its own mind and the ability to dream up new things. A generative AI can create new content that it was never specifically trained on. It doesn't just learn to identify a cat from a dog; it can also generate a completely new image of a cat-dog hybrid if asked. It's like giving the AI a paintbrush, and not only does it replicate the Mona Lisa perfectly, but it also creates its own masterpiece that's just as captivating.

This book has been carefully written to guide you through the details of generative AI. We will traverse its fascinating landscape, venture into its revolutionary applications, and ponder the profound societal changes it could trigger. We will visit art galleries where the artist is an AI, travel through industries it's transforming, and glimpse into classrooms it's reshaping. We will also wrestle with the pressing questions it poses: How will it alter our workforce? What ethical challenges does it present? What security concerns should we consider?

While the implications of generative AI may sound vast and the technology might seem daunting, we will pave this path together in an accessible and engaging way. Each chapter will lead us deeper into the world of generative AI, demystifying its complex mechanics and painting a vivid picture of its potential impacts.

This book is not just for technologists or AI enthusiasts. It's for everyone. It is for anyone wondering about AI's impact on creativity; the entrepreneur seeking opportunities in AI-driven markets; the policymaker pondering AI's ethical and legal implications, and the teacher exploring how AI can enhance education.

As we delve deeper into this book, we are not merely learning about new technology; we are discovering a tool that could shape our future, a catalyst that could redefine our societal, economic, and cultural landscapes. We are not just readers but explorers, pioneers, and possibly the creators of this AI-driven future.

Think of it as standing in front of a door that leads to a place you have never seen before. You are excited and can't wait to see what's on the other side. That's how we are feeling about learning the basics of generative AI. We are just about to step into a future made by combining imagination and intelligence.

2

Dawn of AI

I f you ever wondered about the birth of AI and its evolution
to the stunningly capable and imaginative technology it is
today, we are about to get on board a time travel journey
back to where it all began.

In this chapter, we will explore the humble beginnings of
artificial intelligence, the shifts in AI models that transformed
its capabilities, and the trailblazing journey toward the dawn
of generative AI.

Origins of AI

Our journey begins in the mid-20th century, a time when
computers were enormous, clunky machines, and the idea of
them having a semblance of 'intelligence' was stuff for fantasy
novels.

However, behind the scenes, a revolutionary concept was taking
shape. A group of visionary scientists, including Alan Turing,

were laying the groundwork for what would become artificial intelligence. Turing, a British mathematician, and logician, pondered if machines could mimic human intelligence. His Turing Test, devised in the 1950s, remains a key concept in AI even today. It proposed a simple yet profound idea: if a machine could carry on a conversation such that a human could not distinguish it from another human, then, for all practical purposes, the machine could be considered 'intelligent'.

This notion stirred up a storm in the scientific community. It was both thrilling and terrifying. The possibility of machines thinking like humans nudged us into a new epoch of techno-logical innovation.

In 1956, a remarkable meeting took place at Dartmouth College. John McCarthy, Marvin Minsky, Claude Shannon, and other brilliant minds gathered to tackle the challenge of making machines mimic human intelligence. It was here that the term 'Artificial Intelligence' was coined, setting the stage for a field that would forever change the course of human history.

The early AI models were rule-based, meaning they operated by following explicit instructions provided by human program-mers. These AI systems were a bit like skilled artisans crafting exquisite glassware. Each step was precise, methodical, and carefully controlled. The results were impressive, but they lacked the spontaneity and adaptability inherent to human intelligence. The AI models could perform tasks, but only those for which they were explicitly programmed.

Imagine teaching a child to recognize dogs. You could try to list all the possible characteristics: fur, four legs, a tail, and so on. But what about a dog that's missing a tail, or a breed with short legs? Would the child still recognize them as dogs? Most likely, yes, because human learning is flexible and adaptive and not bound by rigid rules.

This adaptability was what the early AI models lacked. They could follow instructions but struggled with ambiguity and unpredictability. They were like actors who could deliver their lines perfectly on stage but were at a loss if asked to improvise.

This shortcoming marked a pivotal point in AI's journey, a point where the path turned off course and ventured into unknown territories. The pursuit of creating AI that could learn like a human child sparked a new wave of innovation. It was the beginning of a radical transformation in AI models, a transformation that would bring us one step closer to the intelligent, creative AI we're familiar with today.

And as we journey forward in our exploration, we will soon discover how these early models evolved, maturing from rule-following novices to adaptable learners, setting the stage for the birth of generative AI. In the grand tale of artificial intelligence, this is just the introduction. The most exciting chapters are yet to unfold.

Evolution of AI Models

Just like the silent movies of the early 20th century evolved into the immersive IMAX 3D experiences of today, artificial intelligence, too, went through significant transformations.

The rule-based models we discussed earlier were akin to the silent movies—impressive for their time, but constrained by their rigidity and lack of adaptability. But the world of AI was about to experience its 'talkies' moment with the introduction of machine learning.

Machine learning, in essence, gives AI the ability to learn from experience. This was a ground-breaking shift. Instead of teaching computers explicit rules, researchers developed algorithms that allowed computers to learn from data. This was like moving from having to hand-draw every single frame of an animation to being able to create CGI monsters that moved and reacted in realistic ways.

In the case of recognizing dogs, a machine-learning algorithm wouldn't need an exhaustive list of canine characteristics. Instead, it would be shown thousands of dog images, and through learning from these examples, it would understand the distinctive features that make a dog a dog.

The development of machine learning was a pivotal turning point. However, it was not the final destination. Within machine learning, a subfield emerged that would push the boundaries even further, called deep learning. Inspired by the neural networks in our brain, deep learning models, often called artificial neural networks, could handle vast amounts of data, learn from them, and deliver near-human or even superhuman performance in tasks such as image recognition, speech recognition, and natural language processing.

If machine learning was the beginning of the talkies, deep

learning was the dawn of technicolor, adding new dimensions to AI's capabilities. But while deep learning brought AI closer to human-like thinking, it still lacked one crucial aspect: creativity. The AI could learn to recognize patterns, even abstract ones, but it could not create something new or novel.

Imagine being an exceptional art critic, being able to identify the work of every great artist from a single brushstroke. That was what AI could do up to this point. It could recognize Van Gogh's 'Starry Night' from Picasso's 'Guernica'. It could even tell you the key features that distinguish Van Gogh's work from Picasso's. But what it couldn't do was create a new masterpiece that was neither Van Gogh nor Picasso, yet just as stunning.

The aspiration for such creative AI drove the next evolution, steering the journey towards a technology that would blur the line between the human mind's creativity and the cold, calculated precision of AI. A technology that would fuel AI's imagination and, in doing so, open doors to endless possibilities.

The next phase of our exploration leads us toward that horizon, where creativity and artificial intelligence intersect. It's a breathtaking view, a landscape where AI is not merely a mimic but a creator. A territory where AI, like an artist, doesn't just reproduce reality but generates something unique, something novel, something breathtakingly beautiful.

So, let us continue our journey, venturing into the interesting world of generative AI, the AI that imagines and creates, the AI that's not just intelligent but generative. And as we travel this path, remember that we are not just spectators. We are part of this exciting story, a narrative that's scripting the future, one generative AI model at a time.

Path to Generative AI

We stand at the start of AI's latest evolution—the rise of generative models. Imagine an AI not just as a system processing information or learning from patterns but as a creator, a dreamer, if you will, spinning new, unseen patterns from the threads of data it's fed.

This evolution hinged on a fundamental shift in AI's core mechanisms. Rather than simply predicting or classifying, AI has now started generating. Imagine teaching a child about animals. You start with a dog, pointing out its four legs, its tail, and its bark. Over time, you introduce the child to other animals, each with its own unique characteristics. Once the child has seen enough variety, you could show them an outline of a creature they've never seen before and ask them to fill it in, drawing on their knowledge of various animals.

In the world of AI, this child-like imagination found form in Generative Adversarial Networks (GANs), introduced by Ian Goodfellow and his colleagues in 2014. This novel AI framework comprises two neural networks: one to create (the "generator") and another to review (the "discriminator"). The generator is like an eager student creating a piece of art, while the discriminator is the meticulous teacher evaluating the work. This dynamic rivalry pushes the generator to improve and create data that is almost indistinguishable from the real thing.

In the field of images, this could mean generating new faces that don't belong to any existing person yet look convincingly human. For text, it could be writing a story that feels as if a human penned it. The power of GANs and other generative models lies in their ability to understand and capture the essence of the data they're trained on, then use that understanding to create something entirely new.

However, it is crucial to remember that while these models generate, they do not create in the same way humans do. They lack intentionality and understanding. A generative model can paint a picture, but it does not comprehend what a sunset is or why its beauty moves us.

Despite this, the capacity of generative AI is staggering. It's not just about creating realistic faces or generating beautiful music. It's about accelerating drug discovery, personalizing education, designing energy-efficient buildings, and countless other applications that can change the world.

So, as we bring this chapter to a close, it is essential to remember that AI's journey has been a relentless march toward an evolving horizon. We started with machines that followed human-set rules, moved on to AI that learned from data, and have now reached a point where AI can generate new, unseen data. But this is still not the end. It's the beginning of a new day in the world of AI, one filled with even more promise and potential.

As we set our sights on the next chapter, we are about to delve deeper into the fascinating world of generative AI. From understanding how GANs function to exploring transformer models, the technology driving GPT-3 and GPT-4, we will unravel the magic behind AI's creative prowess.

3

The Mechanics of Generative AI

A s we begin this new chapter, imagine yourself as a cryptographer tasked with decoding the most complex of enigmas. Instead of letters and ciphers, you are unraveling the intricate threads of machine learning, neural networks, and Generative Pre-trained Transformer (GPT) models. Our journey now takes us deep into the engine room of generative AI, revealing the gears and pulleys that bring this awe-inspiring technology to life.

In this chapter, we will explore the fundamental mechanics that make generative AI operate. Starting with a dive into the ocean of machine learning, we will learn how these algorithms sift through the currents of data to find precious pearls of insight. Following that, we will climb to the complex networks of artificial neurons, shedding light on the complex connections that give birth to deep learning. Finally, we will journey into the enigmatic world of GPT models, illuminating how these behemoths of AI generate human-like text.

Understanding Machine Learning

Have you ever wondered how a child learns to identify a dog? They start with no knowledge about what a dog is. They don't know its shape, its sound, or its behavior. But through exposure and experience, they start recognizing patterns. They understand that dogs often have four legs, that they bark, and that they wag their tails. This process of learning from data and experience is what lies at the heart of machine learning.

In the AI world, machine learning algorithms are like sponges. They soak up data and learn from it, but instead of identifying dogs or distinguishing apples from oranges, they spot patterns that can help predict stock market trends or diagnose diseases.

Take the case of an AI system designed to predict the weather. It's like a digital meteorologist being fed a ton of data: temperatures, wind speeds, humidity levels, and more from countless locations and times. The AI consumes this data, analyzing and learning from it. It identifies patterns and relationships between different factors. Maybe it notices that a sudden drop in pressure often precedes a storm, or a specific wind pattern could signify an approaching heatwave.

Just like the child learning about dogs, the AI, armed with machine learning, learns from the data. And once it's learned enough, it can start making predictions. Given new data about wind patterns and atmospheric pressure, it can predict if tomorrow will be a sunny day or if you'll need to carry an umbrella.

And that is the essence of machine learning. It's all about learning from data and using that learning to make predictions or decisions. From recommending your next favorite movie to powering self-driving cars, machine learning is at the heart of many modern AI wonders.

Now, picture machine learning as a single neuron in the human brain. On its own, it is capable of remarkable things. But when you start connecting these neurons and building a network, you unlock a whole new level of complexity and capability. This is the threshold we are crossing next. In the next section, we are going to uncover the maze of connections and layers that make up the neural networks, the foundations of deep learning, and the essential gear in the machinery of generative AI.

Decoding Neural Networks

When we start learning about neural networks, it's like stepping into an interesting and complex world. Just as neurons in the human brain connect and communicate to help us make sense of the world, artificial neurons in a neural network collaborate to process complex data, recognize patterns, and make decisions.

Each artificial neuron in the network is like a tiny detective with a magnifying glass, picking up on different aspects of the input data. One might notice a curve, another a straight line, and yet another a specific color. Each neuron specializes in identifying its own pattern in the data, contributing its unique piece to the overall puzzle.

To grasp this, let's consider an example. Suppose we have a neural network trained to recognize handwritten digits. You scribble a '2' on a piece of paper and feed it to the network. The input data here is a grid of pixel values that represents your handwritten '2'. As this information moves through the network, each artificial neuron examines a tiny piece of it and identifies specific features. Some neurons might pick up on the curve at the top, others on the straight line at the bottom. Each neuron passes on its findings to the next layer, which then works to integrate these various features, gradually building up a more comprehensive understanding of the image.

And this isn't a linear process. It is a dynamic, interconnected system where each layer learns to recognize more abstract features based on the findings of the previous layer. Starting from simple patterns such as lines and curves in the early layers, the network gradually builds up to recognizing complex constructs like the digit '2' in the final layers.

This multi-layered, hierarchical approach to learning is what sets neural networks, particularly deep neural networks, apart. It's what enables them to learn from raw, unstructured data and handle tasks of immense complexity, from recognizing objects in images to translating languages and beyond.

However, while this neural network might be great at recognizing handwritten digits, what if we wanted it to generate something new, like a completely new, unseen digit? That's a different ballgame altogether, and it's one that requires an advanced type of AI model. A model that not only learns from data but can generate new data based on its learning.

In this new arena of generative AI, one model has come to the forefront, demonstrating impressive capabilities and transforming the landscape of AI research and application. It's the Generative Pretrained Transformer, or GPT for short, and it's our next stop on this journey. As we prepare to take this leap into the future of AI, hold on to the understanding of machine learning and neural networks we've gained. It will serve as a valuable guidepost as we venture into the world of GPT models and generative AI.

Demystifying GPT Models

With an understanding of machine learning and neural networks, it's time to solve the secrets of GPT models. Imagine them as inventive poets. Instead of simply understanding and translating language, they create it. A GPT model can write an essay, answer questions, or even create a poem from a simple prompt. But how does it pull off this feat?

At the core of a GPT model is a transformative idea: What if we treated the process of understanding the text as a kind of guessing game? Suppose you're reading a sentence that says, "The quick brown fox jumped over the Most people would guess the next word to be lazy," followed by "dog." This is because we have learned this phrase over time and understand the context. GPT models apply this same principle on a much larger scale.

The model is trained on enormous amounts of text data and is tasked with predicting what word comes next based on the words it has seen so far. During this process, the model learns about grammar, facts about the world, and even some reasoning abilities. When it encounters a new prompt, it uses what it has learned to generate a creative and coherent continuation.

Let's put this into context. Suppose we give a GPT model the prompt, "In a world where AI is omnipresent...". The model would then attempt to predict the next word, and the next, until it had spun an entire narrative around the prompt. It could be a dystopian tale about AI taking over the world or a utopia where AI has solved all of humanity's problems. The beauty of GPT models lies in their ability to generate diverse and creative outputs that are contextually appropriate.

The power of GPT models extends beyond just creating text. They are also revolutionizing the way we interact with machines. From AI chatbots to personal assistants, GPT models are making our conversations with AI more natural and intuitive. They're bringing us one step closer to the goal of creating AI that truly understands and interacts with us in a human-like way.

Demystifying the mechanics of generative AI, from the foundations of machine learning to the complexities of GPT models, is like opening a door into a world of untold possibilities. Each discovery, each understanding, is a piece of the puzzle that brings us closer to leveraging this powerful tool to its fullest potential.

We cannot conclude this section without talking about ChatGPT, which revolutionized the AI world when OpenAI made it available to the public in November 2022. Let us learn more about ChatGPT in the next section.

ChatGPT Deep Dive

Think about a friendly chat over a cup of coffee, filled with laughter, interesting stories, and thoughtful discussions. Interestingly, your chat partner could be an AI system called ChatGPT, a type of advanced technology that is reshaping the way we talk with machines.

In the past, communicating with a machine meant dealing with pre-set responses or phrases triggered by certain words. But ChatGPT changes this. It's like a smart, digital friend designed to respond in a way that feels very human, all based on the inputs it gets from us.

ChatGPT is an extensive language model chatbot that was developed by OpenAI. It is a powerful tool that can be used for a variety of tasks, including generating text, translating languages, and writing different kinds of creative content.

ChatGPT is based on the GPT-3 and GPT-4 language models. GPT-3 is a generative pre-trained transformer model that was first announced in June 2020. It has 175 billion parameters, which means that it has been trained on a massive dataset of text and code. GPT-4 is a newer version of GPT-3 that was released in March 2023. It is speculated that GPT-4 uses around 100 trillion parameters, and it has been trained on a dataset that is 10 times larger than the dataset that GPT-3 was trained on.

ChatGPT can generate human-quality text in response to a wide range of prompts and questions. For example, it can provide summaries of factual topics, create stories, and even write different kinds of creative content, like poems, code, scripts, musical pieces, emails, letters, etc. It can also translate languages and answer your questions in an informative way, even if they are open-ended, challenging, or strange.

Although ChatGPT is still under development, it has already been used for a variety of purposes. For example, it has been used to create chatbots that can provide customer service, generate marketing content, and even write scripts for movies and TV shows.

But remember, ChatGPT is not conscious—it does not have beliefs or opinions. Its 'knowledge' and its response are really just a reflection of the data it has been trained on. This mix of processing information and generating language is what makes ChatGPT operate, making it seem like an insightful conversation partner.

ChatGPT is like a complicated mix of math and computer power that shows how far we have come with AI. Its ability to carry a conversation feels impressively human-like, but it's the complex math models and computer processes running in the background that make this possible.

The way ChatGPT works might seem a bit magical and confusing. It is sometimes hard to figure out why it gives certain responses. But this unknown aspect is part of what makes it so interesting and why we are so captivated by these amazing advances in AI.

As ChatGPT continues to develop, it is likely to become

even more powerful and versatile. It has the potential to revolutionize how we interact with computers, create content and effectively help us solve some of the complex business problems.

As we conclude this chapter on the mechanics of generative AI, we will next explore the milestones that have defined this field of technology. Each milestone, each innovation, represents a step forward in our search to unlock the true potential of AI, and it is these steps that will be the focus of our next chapter, "Innovation Milestones."

4

Innovation Milestones

I magine embarking on a thrilling journey back through time, stopping at critical moments that marked the evolution of artificial intelligence. Like pebbles that started an avalanche, these milestones transformed our world in ways unimaginable just a few decades ago.

In this chapter, we will discuss the various milestones of Artificial Intelligence (AI), its most significant turning points, and the various developments. We will delve into the story of its origin, its evolution, and the resulting impact, all of which have helped shape various parts of the AI world. Though we discussed some of these milestones in the previous chapters, this recap helps us gain an understanding of what makes AI a powerful technology that will transform the world and impact the way we live in the years to come.

Landmark Developments in AI

The history of Artificial Intelligence has been quite an exciting ride. As the track unraveled, it brought with it surprise turns, exhilarating climbs, and sudden drops, mirroring the excitement and anticipation of landmark developments in the field. From the genesis of the concept to its maturation into a technological giant, each milestone in the evolution of AI has paved the path toward a future brimming with possibilities.

The term artificial Intelligence' was first coined at the Dartmouth Conference in 1956. During this meeting, a group of ambitious thinkers and visionaries congregated to ponder the idea that every aspect of learning or any other feature of intelligence can be described so accurately that it can be simulated by a machine. This was a pivotal moment—not just a name-giving ceremony but the birth of a revolutionary idea that would forever change the trajectory of technology.

Fast forward to 1980, the year that marked the dawn of the AI winter—a period of disappointment and reduced funding due to the inability of AI to fulfill its promises. Despite the frosty reception, AI, much like a phoenix, rose from its ashes, setting the stage for a resurgence powered by an increasingly digital world and burgeoning data.

The arrival of the Internet started an era of incredible connectivity and a huge increase in data. The machines that once struggled with learning were now being fed a continuous stream of information. This paved the way for machine learning, a significant development where machines could now learn from experience, adjust to inputs, and perform human-like tasks.

The arrival of deep learning changed the game significantly. With multi-layered artificial neural networks, machines started mimicking the human brain, processing data, and creating patterns for decision-making. It could recognize speech, identify images, and even beat the best human player in the game of Go!

As we dwell on these extraordinary milestones, it's interesting to see how each development opens up new frontiers. The AI of today is remarkably different from its ancestor in 1956. From merely simulating human intelligence, it has evolved to understand, learn, and even react like a human brain. It has become an indispensable tool, seamlessly integrating into our daily lives, be it voice assistants, social media algorithms, or email filters.

Our journey into the past has given us an understanding of how AI has transformed, matured, and become part of our daily lives. The story of AI is far from over. We are merely in the face of possibilities, standing on the shoulders of these landmark developments, ready to take the leap into the future. As we look back into history, let us explore the remarkable innovations born out of these developments and how they have reshaped the world around us. After all, the journey of AI is not just about the milestones but also the change they bring forth.

Notable Innovations and Their Impact

Every innovation has a story—a spark that sets off a cascading effect, changing the way we perceive and interact with the world. In the world of Artificial Intelligence, such innovations are not just technological advancements; they are milestones that redefine boundaries and extend the horizons of possibility.

Consider Google's search algorithm. In the early stages, searching the internet was like finding a needle in a haystack. That all changed with Google's PageRank algorithm, an AI innovation that drastically improved the efficiency and accuracy of internet searches. By assessing the relevance of a webpage based on the number and quality of links to it, PageRank revolutionized how we navigate the digital world.

Let us now look at another exciting innovation: self-driving cars. When autonomous vehicles were merely a concept in science fiction, companies like Tesla and Waymo turned that dream into reality. Using AI, they equipped cars with the ability to recognize their surroundings, interpret road signs, and navigate traffic, thereby propelling us toward a future of self-driving vehicles.

Our healthcare system has also felt the evolution of AI. IBM's Watson, an AI system, was used in oncology to provide physicians with evidence-based treatment options. Watson could read and understand natural language, learn from each interaction, and make decisions based on its learning, bringing a new level of precision and personalization to patient care.

Moving to another sector, finance, we have seen the rise of robo-advisors. These AI-powered platforms offer automated, algorithm-based financial advice without the need for human intervention. By taking into account the user's financial situation and future goals, robo-advisors help users make informed investment decisions. This innovation has made financial advice accessible to a broader demographic and steered us into a new era of financial planning.

Each of these remarkable innovations, borne out of AI, has impacted our lives in profound ways. They have reshaped industries, redefined user experiences, and rewritten the rules of what machines are capable of. However, the magic of AI is not confined to high-level innovations alone. Its influence fills everyday life, subtly yet significantly.

To truly appreciate the impact of these groundbreaking innovations, let us bring the spotlight to everyday life. How do these innovations translate to real-world scenarios? How does AI intertwine with our day-to-day experiences? As we move forward, we will dive into a series of case studies that illustrate AI's transformational power, revealing the profound ways in which these technological phenomena continue to shape our world.

Real-World Examples and Case Studies

Our journey through the realm of Artificial Intelligence, laden with impressive innovations, brings us to the heart of the subject: real-world application. It's one thing to marvel at these technological innovations in isolation; it's entirely another to see them in action, weaving their magic into our lives every day.

Think about your typical morning routine. As your alarm rings, it's likely set by a smart assistant like Amazon's Alexa or Google

Home, sophisticated AI entities that streamline our lives. They can not only play our favorite music or tell us the weather, but they can also control smart devices in our homes. The foundation of such smart assistants is AI, incorporating voice recognition and natural language processing, making them more than just robots—they become our personal assistants.

Let's shift our focus to healthcare, where AI has been a game-changer. Take, for instance, the application of AI to detect diabetic retinopathy, a condition that could lead to blindness if left unchecked. Google's DeepMind has developed an AI system capable of analyzing eye scans with a level of accuracy on par with human experts, enabling early detection and treatment.

Next, let's consider the way we shop. When you browse products on e-commerce platforms like Amazon, you will notice a section with recommendations just for you. This personalized touch, powered by AI algorithms, learns from your browsing and purchasing history, improving your shopping experience by suggesting items that align with your preferences.

Switching to entertainment, platforms like Netflix use AI to suggest shows and films you might like based on your viewing history. This AI-driven personalization is a significant reason why we often find ourselves glued to our screens, binge-watching episode after episode.

While these examples provide an understanding of how AI has impacted our daily lives, they represent just the tip of the iceberg. The instances of AI applications are vast and varied, stretching across sectors and impacting lives in profound ways.

As we wrap up this chapter on the significant milestones in AI, we are left with a sense of awe at the transformation it has sparked. The journey through the pages of history to present-day applications has shown us AI's potential and how it has become an integral part of our lives. But the journey of AI innovation is far from over.

Now, with a clear understanding of these significant milestones, we stand poised to plunge into the world of generative AI in action. In the coming chapter, we will explore a relatively uncharted but exciting aspect of AI: its role in art and creativity. We will explore how this powerful technology is not only emulating human intelligence but also displaying a degree of creativity that was once thought to be uniquely human.

5

Generative AI in Art and Creativity

I magine a world where the stroke of a painter's brush is replaced by the calculations of algorithms, where the melody of a song is composed by a computer, and where stories spring from the 'mind' of a machine. That world is no longer a mere figment of our imagination—it's our present, shaped by the astonishing capabilities of generative AI.

As we delve deeper into this chapter, we will unearth the fascinating role of generative AI in the area of art and creativity. We will traverse the landscapes of visual art, music, and literature, where this form of AI has not just made its mark but has also prompted us to reconsider our definition of creativity.

AI in Visual Art

Our exploration begins in the world of visual art, a field where the creative process has been predominantly human for centuries. However, generative AI has burst onto the scene, breathing life into digital canvases in ways we never thought possible.

Imagine standing before a painting, drawn in by its layers of complexity, the play of colors, the story it silently narrates. It looks like the work of a master artist, but it's actually created by an artificial intelligence model. This isn't the future; it's a reality today. For instance, consider the work of the AI model developed by the Paris-based art collective Obvious, named GAN (Generative Adversarial Network). The piece "Portrait of Edmond de Belamy," an AI-generated artwork, stunned the world when it was auctioned for a staggering $432,500 at Christie's in 2018.

But how does it work? Generative AI in visual art leverages machine learning algorithms that 'learn' styles, patterns, and techniques from vast amounts of data—in this case, numerous pieces of art. After training, these algorithms can then generate new artwork that is original yet reminiscent of the styles they have learned.

This capability has spurred a new wave of digital artistry, with AI emerging as a powerful tool in an artist's arsenal. Artists no longer limit themselves to traditional mediums; instead, they are harnessing the power of AI to generate intricate designs, reimagine existing art pieces, or create entirely new works of art that push the boundaries of creativity.

Generative AI has also democratized the world of art. Tools like DeepArt and Artbreeder allow users to transform their photos into artworks, mimicking the styles of famous painters or generating entirely new pieces, no professional artistic skills are required.

However, like every innovation, this evolution comes with questions and debates about the nature of creativity, originality, and the role of AI in the artistic process. These discussions form an essential part of the narrative around AI in visual art, which we will explore in greater detail in the upcoming sections.

We've seen how generative AI is revolutionizing the world of visual art. However, its creative influence doesn't stop there—it has also orchestrated a symphony of innovation in the realm of music.

AI in Music Composition

Just as it has in visual art, AI has also found its rhythm in the realm of music, dancing across the stage to compose melodies that would please even the most discerning of ears. Yes, the art of music composition, which we have long considered to be a testament to human creativity, has welcomed an unexpected player: generative AI.

Let's start by imagining the typical process of composing music. A composer might start with a melody or a rhythm in mind, iterate on it, and build upon it, layering harmonies, and weaving in different instruments. Now, imagine an AI model doing the same. Today, generative AI models are making beautiful music, creating entire compositions from scratch that range from classical symphonies to catchy pop tunes.

But how does it work? To simplify, we can imagine AI as

an extremely observant student. It analyzes copious amounts of music data, learning from the melodic patterns, rhythmic structures, harmonic progressions, and myriad nuances that make a piece of music appealing. Armed with this knowledge, it then generates its own compositions, infused with the styles and elements it has learned.

An excellent example of this is OpenAI's MuseNet, a deep learning model capable of composing music in various genres and styles. Given a few notes or a specific style, MuseNet can generate a full composition that is coherent and often beautiful, offering a tantalizing glimpse into the future of AI-composed music.

And it's not just about creating novel compositions; AI is also being used to complete unfinished works. AIVA (Artificial Intelligence Virtual Artist), an AI model, was tasked with completing Schubert's unfinished Symphony No. 8. The results were astounding—the AI-manufactured section was almost indistinguishable from Schubert's original work.

Yet, these are not mere experiments. AI in music composition is finding practical applications. For example, startups like Jukin and Amper Music use AI to generate copyright-free music for videos, movies, and ads. This development not only saves time but also circumvents licensing issues often associated with using copyrighted music.

The art form we generally associate with soul, emotion, and human touch is now being successfully tackled by artificial intelligence. However, just as in the case of visual art, the role of

AI in music composition invites questions and provokes debate. Some see AI as a tool that can assist artists, while others view it as a potential threat that could supplant human creativity. It's a multifaceted discussion that we will delve into more deeply in this chapter.

AI in Literature and Writing

When it comes to writing, be it weaving a riveting tale or penning a thought-provoking essay, it's hard to imagine anything other than a human behind the masterpiece. Words are deeply connected to our experiences, our emotions, and our very essence. So, can an AI, which lacks all of these, really contribute to literature and writing? The answer, quite surprisingly, is yes.

Let's set the stage by considering the process of writing. A writer usually begins with an idea, an emotion, or a message they want to communicate. Then comes the grueling task of arranging and rearranging words until they paint the perfect picture. With AI, the process begins in much the same way as it does with music composition. In this case, the AI model learns from an enormous amount of text data, grasping the nuances of vocabulary, grammar, and style. Given a prompt or a set of instructions, the AI then generates its own text.

Perhaps the most impressive example of this is the series of AI models developed by OpenAI, including the one you are learning right now, the GPT model. These models, when given a prompt, can write essays, answer questions, and even craft stories that are almost indistinguishable from human-written text. For instance, GPT-3, with its 175 billion parameters, has been used to write articles, poetry, and even a book. Meanwhile, GPT-4 the successor to GPT-3, has been trained on a dataset of text and code that is 100 times larger than the dataset used to train GPT-3. This means that GPT-4 has a massive 170 trillion parameters, which gives it the ability to generate even more creative and informative text than GPT-3.

But AI in writing is not limited to creative ventures alone. In fact, its practical applications are countless. News agencies like the Associated Press and Bloomberg use AI to generate news reports, especially for data-driven topics like sports scores or financial updates. AI is also being used to automate content generation in areas such as product descriptions, email responses, and social media posts.

AI is also transforming the world of editing and proofreading. Tools such as Grammarly use AI to correct grammar, enhance clarity, and suggest style improvements, making the writing process a little less daunting.

There is no denying that the footprints of AI are evident across the terrain of literature and writing. And as technology evolves, these footprints are set to become deeper and more widespread.

So, we have journeyed through the world of art, danced to the rhythm of AI-composed music, and marveled at the prose and poetry penned by artificial intelligence. We've seen how generative AI is not just mimicking human creativity but adding a unique touch of its own, creating a fusion of art and science that's truly fascinating.

In the next chapter, we shift gears from the realm of art and creativity to explore how generative AI is making waves in a rather different landscape - the world of business and economy. We will discover how AI is disrupting industries, driving innovation, and creating new markets.

6

Generative AI's Influence on Business and Economy

When you think of disruption, it may often carry a negative meaning—something that unsettles the status quo or interrupts a calm flow. However, when we talk about disruptions in business and the economy, particularly those spurred by generative AI, they are incredibly exciting. These disruptions are game-changers, redefining how we operate, produce, and deliver, carving the path for innovation and new markets.

Disruption in Traditional Industries

For a moment, the word "factory" may evoke images of bustling production lines, clattering machinery, and hard-working individuals hunched over their workstations. But imagine a different scene: a quiet factory with machines communicating silently, self-diagnosing problems, scheduling maintenance, and even ordering spare parts. All the while, products are customized to individual customer specifications, thanks to

AI-powered production systems. Welcome to the world of smart manufacturing, a glaring example of how generative AI disrupts traditional industries.

Another industry that is undergoing a significant AI-induced transformation is healthcare. AI is not only assisting in diagnosing diseases with remarkable precision but also personalizing treatment plans based on an individual's genetic makeup. Deep learning models are trained to read radiological images and detect anomalies that might be overlooked by the human eye. Predictive analytics powered by AI help identify at-risk patients, allowing for early intervention.

In the world of finance, robotic advisors are making personalized financial advice accessible to the masses. These digital platforms, guided by AI, offer automated, algorithm-driven financial planning services with minimal human supervision. From curating a diversified investment portfolio to tax-loss harvesting, these robotic advisors are democratizing finance like never before.

Even agriculture, one of the oldest industries, is not immune to the disruptive influence of AI. Precision agriculture employs AI-driven technologies to monitor crop health, predict weather patterns, optimize irrigation, and manage resources. It is transforming agriculture from a labor-intensive sector to a data-driven, efficient industry.

We have seen how the invisible hand of generative AI is gently nudging traditional industries toward transformation. But that is just the tip of the iceberg. As the AI wave continues to surge, its ripple effect is felt far and wide, paving the way for unprecedented innovation. In the next section, let us explore how generative AI is driving innovation.

Driving Innovation

As we navigate the landscape of generative AI in the world of business and economy, the phrase "driving innovation" constantly echoes around us. In its essence, driving innovation is about promoting an environment that encourages creativity, allowing for the development of new processes, products, or even entire business models that redefine how we operate. Let's now delve into this fascinating aspect of AI, peeling back layers to reveal how AI is pushing the boundaries and propelling us into a future filled with limitless possibilities.

Take a moment and think about the last time you used a ride-hailing app. As you tap a few buttons on your screen, complex algorithms come to life. AI sifts through a multitude of data points—your location, the availability of drivers, and traffic conditions—to connect you with a driver who will pick you up in a matter of minutes. It's an everyday example of how AI-driven innovation is transforming traditional business models, making them more efficient, consumer-friendly, and sustainable.

This kind of innovation is not just limited to the world of consumer applications. The fields of supply chain management and logistics are undergoing similar transformations. Consider the advent of autonomous trucks, for instance. These vehicles use advanced AI algorithms to navigate roads, adjust to traffic conditions, and deliver goods safely and efficiently. This not only streamlines logistics operations but also addresses pressing issues such as driver shortages and high labor costs.

AI is also fueling innovation in the world of customer service. Thanks to AI-powered chatbots, businesses can provide around-the-clock customer support, handling common queries, and providing immediate responses. This not only improves customer satisfaction but also reduces operational costs for businesses.

In the field of product development, AI-powered predictive analytics tools are revolutionizing how businesses forecast demand, manage inventory, and launch new products. These tools analyze vast amounts of data, identify patterns, and provide precise predictions, enabling businesses to make data-driven decisions, reduce waste, and improve efficiency.

This culture of AI-driven innovation is not a matter of choice anymore—it's a necessity for businesses to stay competitive and relevant in a rapidly evolving market landscape. As we embrace this culture, an interesting phenomenon is unfolding right before our eyes. The widespread adoption of AI is creating an array of unique opportunities and niches that were nonexistent a few years ago, giving birth to entirely new markets.

We are just beginning to explore this new world created by AI's innovative expertise. As we move to the next section, we will dive into these unknown territories, the new markets created by generative AI. These are spaces where imagination and innovation collide to shape a future that is as thrilling as it is unpredictable.

Creating New Markets

As we examine the broad impact of AI on business and the economy, we encounter an interesting perspective. Here, AI is not merely improving existing systems; it is also building completely new structures and establishing new markets. Prepare yourself, focus, and be ready to discover the exciting ways in which AI is not just a part of the economy but is completely transforming it.

Think about the rise of AI-based fitness coaching apps, for instance. Instead of hiring a personal coach or subscribing to a gym, users can now get personalized training regimens, diet plans, and health monitoring right on their smartphones. It's not merely a shift from physical to digital; it is the creation of a new market entirely, enabled by AI's ability to tailor fitness programs for each individual based on their specific goals, abilities, and progress.

Or consider AI's intervention in the domain of mental health. Mobile applications offering AI-powered mental health support, such as virtual cognitive-behavioral therapy, have created a new industry. They make mental health services accessible to a much larger population anytime, anywhere, thereby opening a previously untapped market.

Another fascinating example is AI's venture into the domain of language translation and learning. The ability to translate text or even voice in real time has opened up avenues for business expansion, tourism, and global communication that were previously restricted by language barriers. Additionally, AI-powered language learning platforms offer personalized learning experiences, breaking away from traditional one-size-fits-all language courses, and carving a unique niche in the education market.

As we navigate through these new markets, it becomes increasingly clear that they share a common thread. They are all results of AI's capacity to personalize, understand individual needs, and adapt accordingly. This ability is fundamental to the creation of these new markets, as it allows for the provision of customized solutions on a mass scale.

While we wonder about AI's ability to create new markets, it is critical to understand the problems it poses. Issues of data privacy, the digital divide, and the need for regulatory oversight loom large, necessitating robust discussions and thoughtful policymaking.

Creating new markets is a vibrant and important thread in the broad variety of generative AI's effects on business and the economy. As we finish this chapter, we will next look at the worlds of education and research to see how AI is transforming these disciplines. AI's influence is enormous and transformational, from classrooms to cutting-edge labs.

7

Generative AI in Education and Research

J ust as a magnifying glass can help us see the intricate details of a leaf, or a telescope can reveal the wonders of distant galaxies, we are now prepared to explore an exhilarating new frontier. This time, our lens is artificial intelligence, and our exciting expedition leads us into the heart of education and research.

In this chapter, we will dive into how AI is redefining the landscape of education and scientific research. We will explore how AI is revolutionizing teaching and learning, increasing knowledge accessibility, and driving scientific progress at a breathtaking pace.

AI in Teaching and Learning

Imagine a classroom where there are no dusty chalkboards or stern-faced teachers. Instead, you have a digital space, filled with lively engagement, personalized attention, and boundless exploration. Here, AI is the guide, nudging learners forward, and tailoring the path to suit each unique journey. This is the world of AI in teaching and learning.

As we walk through this digital classroom, we are greeted first by adaptive learning platforms. No two learners are the same, so why should their lessons be? AI-driven platforms can analyze a learner's strengths and weaknesses, adapt content in real time, and provide personalized learning paths. For instance, consider an AI tutoring system that could provide additional challenges to a student who quickly grasps algebra but take a slower, more illustrative approach to a student who struggles.

Next, we meet AI-powered gamified learning platforms, which are transforming the way subjects are taught and learned. Ever thought learning to code could be as engaging as playing a video game? That's exactly what platforms such as CodeCombat and CodinGame have accomplished. They use AI to offer a tailored, immersive learning experience that makes even complex subjects like programming a fun adventure.

The AI teaching assistant also has a prominent place in our AI-powered classroom. Students often hesitate to ask questions in a large class, but an AI teaching assistant, available 24/7, ensures that every question is answered, and every doubt clarified. Universities like Georgia Tech have already seen outstanding success with their AI teaching assistant, Jill Watson.

Lastly, we see AI shaping learning beyond the world of academia. Social-emotional learning, a critical part of education often overlooked in traditional classrooms, can be promoted by AI-driven platforms. They can help learners understand and manage emotions, build empathy, and make sound decisions.

As we exit the virtual classroom, we can't help but marvel at the transformation AI is driving in teaching and learning. It's personal, engaging, and comprehensive, enabling learners to break free from the one-size-fits-all approach of traditional education.

Yet, the power of AI extends beyond the realms of teaching and learning. It carries the potential to democratize knowledge and bring learning opportunities to those who were previously denied. As we move to the next section, we delve deeper into how AI is making knowledge accessible to all, thereby shattering barriers and empowering learners across the globe.

Making Knowledge Accessible

As we continue our exploration of generative AI's influence, we find ourselves in a vast, diverse landscape where knowledge isn't just for the privileged few, but rather a shared treasure accessible to all. This part of our journey illuminates how AI plays a crucial role in socializing knowledge.

Imagine a world where educational opportunities aren't constrained by geographical boundaries, where learning is not a privilege but a right accessible to all. That is the world AI is helping shape. Online platforms powered by AI, like Khan Academy and Coursera, are making high-quality education accessible to millions globally, leveling the educational playing field. With personalized, adaptive learning paths and a variety of courses from top-tier universities, these platforms are a testament to AI's power to democratize knowledge.

Furthermore, AI-powered language translation tools, such as Google Translate, are breaking language barriers in education. Today, a student in Argentina can easily access a research paper published in German or a French e-learning course that can be understood by learners in Japan. Take "DeepL," an AI-based tool, that can translate texts to and from 26 languages with surprising accuracy, helping people around the world access knowledge previously locked behind the language barrier. With AI bridging language gaps, the breadth and depth of accessible knowledge are truly global.

Another major stride in democratizing knowledge is the use of AI to make educational resources accessible to differently abled individuals. Text-to-speech technology helps visually impaired individuals access written content, while speech-to-text aids the hearing impaired. Such AI-powered accessibility tools are playing an invaluable role in creating inclusive learning environments.

However, the widespread availability and accessibility of knowledge isn't limited to just education. We see its powerful impact in the sphere of news and information as well. AI algorithms are helping ensure the spread of quality, fact-checked information, countering the flood of misinformation on digital platforms. Initiatives like the AI-powered fact-checker, Factmata, are empowering users to differentiate between credible news and fake narratives.

AI's influence extends to legal knowledge as well, with AI-driven platforms providing free legal advice, making an often complicated and costly domain more accessible. The AI chatbot, DoNotPay, for instance, provides a service called "robot lawyer" that helps users fight parking tickets, navigate the legalities of small claims court, and much more.

As we meander through the many ways AI is socializing knowledge, we can't help but marvel at the profound impact it's having. It's breaking down barriers, expanding horizons, and making the world a more equitable place.

As we take a step further, we are about to delve into a world where AI isn't just making existing knowledge accessible but is also actively contributing to the creation of new knowledge. We will now venture into the exciting domain of AI and how it accelerates scientific research. This is a space where AI reads, learns, hypothesizes, experiments, and even discovers, reshaping the future of scientific progress.

Accelerating Scientific Research

Let us jump into an exciting domain buzzing with revolutionary discoveries and monumental leaps of understanding. Here, generative AI becomes a powerhouse, a turbo-boost for accelerating scientific research.

Just picture the immense universe of scientific literature. An average researcher could spend a lifetime attempting to parse through it all, only to have new research continuously added at a rapid pace. Generative AI, however, can consume, analyze, and summarize thousands of scientific papers in a fraction of the time, pointing researchers to relevant studies and potential breakthroughs. In this domain, a project like Semantic Scholar, developed by the Allen Institute for AI, stands out. It uses AI to help scientists stay up-to-date with the latest research, effectively cutting through information overload.

Next, let us envision the massive datasets used in various scientific fields. Manually analyzing such data could take years and potentially yield more questions than answers. Generative AI can not only process these datasets swiftly, but it can also spot patterns and correlations that a human might miss. A stellar example of this is Google's DeepMind, whose AlphaFold program revolutionized protein folding research for its ability to accurately predict the structure of proteins, potentially fast-tracking developments in understanding diseases and drug discovery. In fact, AlphaFold was used to predict the structure of the SARS-CoV-2 spike protein, which is the protein that the virus uses to enter cells. This information was very useful in developing new vaccines and treatments for COVID-19.

Imagine the complex scientific models—the kind that requires immense computational power and time to solve. Generative AI can generate and evaluate numerous models concurrently, significantly speeding up the process. One instance is climate modeling, where AI is used to create faster, more accurate models, offering better predictions and insights about our changing climate.

Then, consider the painstaking lab experiments, repeated endlessly until a discovery is made. Generative AI can simulate these experiments, predict outcomes, and even suggest new avenues of inquiry. Take IBM's RoboRXN for Chemistry, which uses AI to predict chemical reactions, helping researchers design new drugs without the need for extensive lab testing.

Finally, think of the difficult process of innovation itself. It's a path filled with trials and errors, hunches, and hypotheses. Generative AI can produce a myriad of novel ideas, innovations, and solutions, challenging and expanding the frontiers of human imagination. DeepArt.io, for instance, uses AI to create new art forms, challenging our perception of creativity, and potentially sparking a wave of innovation in the art world.

In this vibrant arena of scientific research, generative AI emerges as an indispensable ally, a tireless companion, and a catalyst, sparking an explosion of knowledge and innovation.

But as we marvel at these wonders, it is essential to remember that every technological leap comes with societal implications. It's like throwing a stone in a calm pond; the ripples spread out, touching every aspect of our lives. Generative AI is no different. Its impact extends beyond the world of education and research, reaching into the social part of our lives, and transforming how we work and live.

Our thrilling adventure keeps going as we look ahead at these fresh prospects, expecting the intricate changes that generative AI is bringing into our lives. Now let us explore how generative AI is creating a monumental impact in the healthcare sector.

8

Generative AI and Healthcare

I magine a world where a disease is diagnosed before it even begins to show symptoms, where medical treatment plans are customized to each patient's unique genetic makeup, and where new drugs are discovered at a pace, previously thought impossible. This is not a sci-fi novel plot; it's the world being shaped by Generative AI in healthcare.

In this chapter, we will explore the transformational impact of Generative AI in the healthcare sector. From revolutionizing diagnostics and treatment to accelerating drug discovery and bespoke medicine, AI is rapidly ushering in a new era of health and wellness. Yet, along with these exciting developments come ethical dilemmas and challenges that require careful consideration.

Transforming Diagnostics and Treatment

Everyone in healthcare is talking about 'Generative AI'. It's like we have a new magician in town who is using exciting tricks to make big changes. It's a topic that is interesting because of how much it can change things, starting with how we diagnose and treat illnesses.

When you fall sick, the first step is to diagnose what is causing the illness. This process has not changed much over the years. You visit a doctor, and they ask you questions, conduct physical exams, and order tests. Based on the results, they figure out the problem and plan your treatment. It's a time-tested process, but it's far from perfect. Misdiagnoses occur, treatments can fail, and precious time is lost.

Here's where generative AI can make a huge impact. Imagine a system that can scan through thousands, even millions, of medical records in the blink of an eye. A system that can spot patterns and draw insights that even the most experienced doctors might miss. This is not some future fantasy. It's happening now, and it's changing how we diagnose illnesses.

For instance, consider medical imaging. It's an essential tool for diagnosing various conditions. However, interpreting these images requires expertise and time. Generative AI systems can analyze these images, learning from countless previous examples to spot the tell-tale signs of diseases such as cancer. These systems can assist doctors by highlighting areas of concern and reducing the chance of oversight.

But the magic of AI does not stop at diagnosis. Once we know what's wrong, AI can help determine the best course of action. Each of us is unique, and our bodies respond differently to treatments. AI can analyze a person's medical history, genetics, and even lifestyle factors to suggest the most effective treatment. This personalized approach can potentially increase treatment success rates and reduce side effects.

Generative AI, with its ability to learn and generate new data, can also help forecast how a patient's condition might progress and how they might respond to different treatments. This kind of predictive analysis can help doctors make more informed decisions.

The impact of generative AI on diagnostics and treatment is profound. It's like having a super-intelligent assistant that can crunch through vast amounts of data, spot patterns, make predictions, and provide personalized recommendations. It's not here to replace doctors but to enhance their abilities and provide them with tools to make better, more informed decisions.

With AI's growing role in diagnostics and treatment, it's easy to see why there's so much excitement about its potential. However, the story of AI's impact on healthcare doesn't end here. As powerful as these tools are, they are just the beginning. From here, we will dive into another groundbreaking area where AI is making waves - the field of drug discovery and personalized medicine.

Revolutionizing Drug Discovery and Personalized Medicine

Traditionally, the development of new drugs takes years, if

not decades, of research, experiments, trials, and a significant amount of resources. It's a process to find that elusive compound that can treat a disease without causing harm. The process is slow, expensive, and filled with failures. But Generative AI can help speed things up, make it more efficient, and reduce the rate of failure. This is revolutionizing drug discovery and the concept of personalized medicine.

Let us explore the world where biology meets advanced computing. Generative AI has a unique ability: it can generate new data after learning from existing data. In the context of drug discovery, this 'existing data' is the vast database of known drugs and their structures, along with biological information about different diseases. Generative AI can scan through this information, learn from it, and then generate new potential drug molecules.

It is not a random process, but a calculated, intelligent process that takes into account various factors such as the desired properties of the drug, its potential side effects, its effectiveness against a specific disease, and even its manufacturing process. What usually takes years of human effort, AI can do in a matter of days or weeks.

Now, let us add another layer to this: personalized medicine. Generative AI is not just about finding new drugs; it's also about tailoring treatments to individual patients. Everyone is different; our bodies, our genes, and our lifestyles are all unique. These differences can affect how we respond to drugs.

By analyzing a person's genetic data, lifestyle factors, and disease history, generative AI can suggest a personalized treatment plan. It can predict which drugs would be most effective, what dosage should be administered, and even anticipate potential side effects. It's like having a personalized treatment plan, designed specifically for you!

Imagine the possibilities. Faster drug discovery, more effective treatments, less trial-and-error, and personalized healthcare! It's like a new revolution in the world of medicine because of the power of generative AI.

However, the integration of AI into healthcare brings its own share of ethical considerations and challenges. So, as we marvel at the wonders of generative AI in healthcare, let us also explore these concerns. This is an important aspect because understanding the full picture is crucial to harnessing the power of AI responsibly.

Ethical Considerations and Challenges

Our journey so far has been an exploration into the marvels of generative AI, its capabilities, and its transformational potential in healthcare. But, as with any powerful tool, it's crucial to balance its use with careful consideration of ethics and potential challenges. AI, when wielded thoughtlessly, could raise questions that stir the very core of our values and morality.

Imagine being in a situation where an AI model recommends a treatment that goes against a patient's preferences or cultural beliefs. Or, consider a scenario where personalized treatment plans created by AI are only accessible to those who can afford them, widening the already existing health disparity gap. These are just a few instances where ethical concerns come into play.

AI's role in healthcare is not just about providing benefits; it's also about ensuring these benefits are fair and accessible and respecting our diverse human values. Decisions in healthcare, more than in any other field, have extreme implications. They often involve life-altering, sometimes life-ending outcomes, and these decisions must be guided by ethical principles.

The inclusion of generative AI in healthcare also presents a unique set of challenges. One significant challenge is data privacy. The AI models need vast amounts of data for training, and this data often includes sensitive personal information. How do we ensure this data is protected? How do we navigate the tricky waters of data privacy without limiting the benefits of AI?

Another challenge is understanding how AI makes its decisions. AI models, especially those based on deep learning, are often called "black boxes" due to their complexity. If we are to trust AI with critical health decisions, we need to make these "black boxes" more transparent.

In our exploration of generative AI in healthcare, we have looked into a future filled with potential and promise, but not without its issues. The task ahead is to understand these concerns better, navigate the challenges responsibly, and find a balance that respects our ethics while also leveraging the power of AI.

Now, let us shift our attention from the healthcare sector to a domain that touches our lives in a completely different way: the world of entertainment. Just as in healthcare, the ripple effects of AI are transforming this space in ways we could only imagine a few years ago. Let us discuss in the next chapter, where creativity meets code and the lines between reality and simulation blur.

9

AI's Imprint on Entertainment

C an you imagine a world where artificial intelligence crafts our favorite songs, directs blockbuster films, and even designs immersive video games? This new age of entertainment is quite possible because it is shaped and molded by the hand of AI.

This chapter aims to take you on a journey into the heart of the entertainment industry, exploring how AI technology is leaving its unique imprint and reshaping our experiences.

AI and Content Creation

Imagine getting lost in an amazing movie, a catchy song, or an engaging video game. You forget about everything else and just dive into this world of stories, sounds, and feelings. From the unexpected story to the tunes you can't get out of your head, everything might actually be created by artificial intelligence.

In today's entertainment industry, AI isn't just a tool; it's a revolutionary game-changer, a co-creator working side by side with human artists, bringing stories, sounds, and worlds to life. It is the unseen hand shaping your entertainment experiences in ways you may never have realized.

When we talk about movies, the importance of AI can't be overstated. It's there in the pre-production stages, aiding in script writing by analyzing patterns and structures from successful movies, predicting plot trends, and even suggesting character arcs. It's there in post-production too, helping in editing by trimming down hours of footage into streamlined narratives, optimizing color correction, and even generating realistic CGI effects.

Even music is being rewritten or composed by AI. We are not just talking about recommendations on streaming plat-forms—that's old news. AI is actively involved in the creation of music itself. From melody generation to harmonizing and even producing lyrics, artificial intelligence tools have been assisting artists to create unique, captivating pieces. Popgun's AI named 'Alice' is an example that can improvise a jazz solo in real-time, just like a human musician.

Let us take a moment and dive into the magical world of gaming. If you have played a video game recently, you have interacted with AI. Whether it's the NPCs (Non-Player Characters) you encounter, the enemies you fight, or the evolving game world around you, AI is the driving force behind it all. It crafts engaging, responsive environments and characters that enhance the gaming experience. The AI in 'F.E.A.R.' is well regarded for its tactical decision-making skills, providing a thrilling challenge for the player.

As we explore the landscape of AI in entertainment, it is essential to recognize that AI is not here to replace the creative instincts and passion of human artists. Instead, it acts as a tool, an aid that expands the realm of what's possible. Just as a paintbrush does not paint on its own, AI also needs the guiding hand of a creative mind to truly bring art to life.

With AI's impact deep in the heart of content creation, a question arises about how this is affecting us as an audience. The impact of AI doesn't stop at its creation; it ripples outward, influencing how we experience and interact with entertainment.

AI's Impact on Viewer Experience and Industry Evolution

Just as a pebble tossed into a lake sends ripples spreading across the water, the influence of AI in the entertainment industry doesn't stop at creation; it extends to transforming the way we, the audience, experience the magic. It's in every recommended show on Netflix, every song suggested on Spotify and every immersive game world that adapts to our choices. This chapter explores the impact of AI on our entertainment experiences and how it's reshaping the industry.

Consider this, the next time you find yourself immersed in a binge-worthy Netflix series, AI is involved there. The streaming giant utilizes advanced algorithms to analyze your viewing patterns, compare them with those of millions of other users, and recommend shows you are likely to enjoy. This provides

Personalized entertainment at its finest. Your Netflix homepage is as unique as your fingerprints, catering to your specific tastes, and enhancing your viewing experience.

This personalized experience extends to music, too. Spotify's Discover Weekly, with its uncannily accurate music recommendations, is a perfect example. The platform's sophisticated algorithms analyze your listening habits and compare them with those of similar users to suggest songs you haven't heard but will probably love. It's like having a personal DJ who knows your musical interests better than you do!

The effect of AI on the viewer experience is not just about personalization. It's about enrichment. In gaming, AI-powered physics engines and AI-driven Non-Player Characters (NPCs) contribute to more realistic, engaging, and immersive gaming experiences. For instance, in Red Dead Redemption 2, each NPC has its own daily routine, reacts to the player's actions, and the game world evolves based on player decisions, thanks to complex AI algorithms.

Let us explore how this is influencing the evolution of the entertainment industry. For starters, the surge in personalized content is increasing viewer engagement and satisfaction, leading to customer loyalty. Businesses in the entertainment sector are leveraging AI to optimize their offerings and drive growth. With AI, they can make informed decisions about which projects to green light, who might enjoy them, and how to market them effectively. For instance, Warner Bros. employed AI to analyze audience preferences and box-office trends to make better investment decisions.

Moreover, the intersection of AI and entertainment is opening new avenues for creativity and innovation. AI is not just a tool; it's a collaborative partner pushing the boundaries of what's possible. It is enabling artists to experiment and innovate, leading to a rich diversity of content. For instance, Taryn Southern, an artist, used Amper AI, an AI music composer, to create an entire album, marking a new milestone in the world of music.

But it's not just about AI. The human element — our creativity, our emotions, and our subjective interpretations — is what breathes life into art and entertainment. The true beauty lies in the dance between human creativity and artificial intelligence, a dance that is shaping the future of entertainment. And that is exactly what we are about to explore next — the fascinating interaction between human artists and their increasingly capable AI partners.

The Dance between Human Creativity and AI

Dance is a beautifully orchestrated sequence of movements, a blend of individual creativity and practiced skill. But can the dance floor accommodate an unexpected partner, artificial intelligence? In the world of entertainment, this unusual combination is not just a fanciful dream but a blossoming reality. This section explores the fascinating interaction of human creativity and AI in the creation of novel and riveting art forms.

An artist's playground is huge. It's not just about painting or drawing but also includes making movies, composing music, writing stories, and so much more. Consider painting, for instance. The Brushstroke app enables users to convert their photos into stunning paintings in the style of famous artists. But, instead of simply applying filters, the AI analyzes the image and the chosen style and recreates the picture from scratch, like a digital artist.

In literature, AI assists human authors in crafting compelling narratives. AI models, trained on vast text datasets, can generate creative text that captures a writer's style. It's not about AI replacing authors but providing them with a tool to stimulate their imagination and overcome writer's block. In 2018, an AI program called "Shelley" co-wrote horror stories with human collaborators, presenting a unique blend of human and artificial creativity.

Movies, too, are becoming a playground for AI's creative experiments. Scripts for short films like "Sunspring" and "It's No Game" were penned by an AI named Benjamin. While these films may not be Oscar-worthy yet, they offer a fascinating glimpse into the potential of AI in screenwriting.

In the domain of music, AI is not just composing background scores, but also creating entirely new pieces. AIVA (Artificial Intelligence Virtual Artist), an AI composer, has been officially recognized as a composer by the French Authors Society. AIVA learns from the compositions of great maestros and creates original music, marrying centuries of human creativity with AI's processing power.

This symbiotic relationship between human creativity and

AI is reshaping the entertainment industry. It's not about humans versus machines, but rather about humans working with machines to explore new horizons of creativity. This fusion is leading to a whole new paradigm of co-creation that's exciting, liberating, and filled with endless possibilities.

Wrapping up this chapter, let us acknowledge this impressive partnership. It's a collaboration where human ingenuity ignites the spark of creativity and passion, and AI steps in to amplify and shape these ideas into reality. This partnership is not just transforming entertainment; it is also prompting us to rethink the limits of art and creativity.

However, as AI circles around virtually every aspect of our lives, it is important to consider its broader implications.

Our thrilling adventure keeps going as we look ahead at these fresh prospects, expecting the intricate changes that generative AI is bringing into our lives. Now let us explore how technology interacts with society and understand how generative AI affects jobs and employment.

10

Generative AI - Changing the Face of Work

Technology is like a changing wave; it always moves and alters our society in strong and sometimes surprising ways. Now, we are at the beginning of a new period highlighted by the growth of generative AI. We are about to see big changes in the workplace that will be as influential as the industrial revolution.

In this chapter, we will explore these changes in detail. We will look at how generative AI is transforming various job sectors and influencing employment patterns. We will also discuss the possible challenges and opportunities this presents to workers and employers alike. We will also explore the reality of job displacement due to automation, the new employment opportunities that AI can create, and how the fundamental nature of work might change in an AI-driven world.

Job Displacement

Picture the assembly lines of the early 20th century, the rhythmic sound of machines, and the toiling workers keeping pace with the ceaseless churn of technology. Then, imagine the scene slowly transforming. The human figures start to fade. Robots, managed and controlled by increasingly sophisticated AI systems, fill the frame. This is not some dismal vision of the future. It is a glimpse into the current reality of many industries worldwide, and it marks a significant trend: job displacement due to AI.

As generative AI becomes more advanced, its ability to automate tasks is spreading beyond physical labor in factories to include knowledge-based work. Lawyers, doctors, writers, and even programmers could find aspects of their work being done faster, more efficiently, and at a lower cost by AI. For example, legal AI software can now review contracts and case law, tasks that once consumed countless hours of a lawyer's time.

People who are now employed in these positions may need to retrain or find other work. The displacement effect can be alarming. Workers may find themselves in the unnerving position of having to compete with machines that don't need breaks, healthcare, or even a salary. While AI can perform specific tasks very well, it doesn't have the same broad adaptability, creative problem-solving abilities, and emotional intelligence as humans.

Nevertheless, job displacement due to AI isn't a threat that can be ignored. It's a trend that requires careful thinking and planning at all levels of society, from individual career choices to public policy decisions. Retraining and upskilling initiatives could help workers adapt to and thrive in an AI-driven job market. While the journey might be challenging, the end goal—a workforce equipped with the skills of the future - is worth striving for.

As we move forward, let us not forget to look back at the lessons from history. The industrial revolution, the advent of computers, and the internet era—each wave of technological advancement has led to job displacement. On the bright side, these revolutions also gave birth to new jobs, new industries, and new opportunities—a phenomenon we will explore in the next section.

Job Creation

In the big story of history, technology has always played a major role. It changes things, sometimes removing old ways, but always bringing in new ones. When we discuss AI and jobs, it's easy to worry about the scary story of people losing jobs and having fewer work chances. But let's also think about the positive side. The side that makes new jobs even while it makes old ones automatic. This is the world of jobs created by AI.

While AI has the potential to make certain roles obsolete, it also has the inherent capacity to create new ones. For example, consider the automotive industry. As self-driving cars become more prevalent, we may need fewer drivers. However, there will be an increase in demand for AI specialists who can maintain and improve these autonomous systems. Similarly, in the healthcare sector, while AI can analyze patient data and suggest diagnoses, it creates roles for healthcare professionals who can understand and interpret these findings, providing a human touch in their delivery.

There are jobs we cannot even imagine as of today, jobs that will only emerge as AI evolves and penetrates various sectors of our economy. These could range from AI ethics managers responsible for ensuring that AI applications adhere to ethical guidelines, to personal data brokers, who help individuals manage and monetize their digital footprints. The beginning of AI is not simply about robots replacing humans, but rather about humans working with AI in ways that can push the boundaries of innovation and productivity.

However, it is essential to acknowledge that this job creation aspect of AI isn't a magic bullet that will automatically balance out the jobs lost to automation. The skills needed for the new jobs might differ vastly from those becoming obsolete. A truck driver cannot simply transition overnight to an AI specialist role without considerable reskilling and training. Hence, it's crucial to have initiatives and strategies in place that can help workers navigate these transitions and ensure that the benefits of AI-driven job creation are equitably distributed.

In this era of AI and automation, we are not just passive spectators; we are actors on this stage, and our actions can shape the script. By embracing lifelong learning and fostering adaptability, we can turn the AI challenge into an opportunity, a springboard to launch us into careers that are not just resilient in the face of AI but are enabled and enriched by it.

As we conclude the discussion on AI and job creation, it rises again to reveal yet another transformation. Beyond creating and displacing jobs, AI stands ready to redefine the very nature of work itself. Let us discuss this in the next section.

Changes to the Nature of Work

As we continue to explore the changing world of AI and its impact on jobs, we find ourselves adjusting our perspectives. We have discussed job losses and the birth of new roles, but now we are arriving at the most thought-provoking part of our exploration. We are not only talking about how the old jobs are being replaced by new ones, but also about how the nature of the work is undergoing a major transformation. This is the point where AI begins to change not just our duties, but also how we perform them. Let us discuss more about how AI can reshape the nature of the work we do day in and day out.

Before we dive deeper, let us take a step back and picture a traditional workplace. You may envision a bustling office teeming with people hunched over desks, attending meetings, and engaging in water cooler conversations. You might think of the clock ticking 9-to-5, of the commute, of the physical presence and interaction. Now, let us add the flavor of AI to this picture.

Suddenly, the office isn't just a physical space anymore. Remote work becomes not just possible, but efficient and productive, thanks to AI-powered collaboration tools. The 9-to-5 clock blurs as AI automation takes over routine tasks, freeing us to work at our own pace and during peak productivity hours. The boundaries of the workplace start to dissolve, replaced by a digital, flexible, and AI-enhanced work environment.

However, this transformation is not without its challenges. With AI taking over routine tasks, the spotlight is now firmly on skills that are uniquely human. Creativity, problem-solving, and emotional intelligence - are the crucial aspects of this new world. This shift necessitates a radical rethink of our education and training systems, which have traditionally focused more on technical skills and rote learning.

Moreover, as AI continues to augment our capabilities, we find ourselves walking a delicate tightrope. On one side, we have the potential for greatly improved productivity and personalization. On the other side, we face potential pitfalls related to over-reliance on AI, erosion of personal privacy, and concerns about AI decision-making transparency.

As we wrap up this section about the impacts of generative AI on work and employment, it becomes clear that we are not merely passive observers, instead, we hold the pen that writes this story. Through informed decisions, we can steer the course of AI in a way that maximizes its benefits while mitigating its challenges.

In this chapter, we discussed everything from job displacement to job creation, finally landing us in the midst of major changes to the very nature of work. The impacts of AI, however, extend beyond the world of work. As we dive into our next chapter, we will discuss the challenging topic of ethics and regulation, which will throw open the doors to a whole new set of intriguing questions and possibilities.

11

Ethical Challenges in Generative AI

In a world where technology surpasses human intelligence, influencing our lives, society, and future with its decisions, it becomes necessary to determine the authority that sets the standards of right and wrong for an artificial mind.

In this chapter, we will explore the nature of AI ethics—the principles that govern the behavior of AI systems, and the guidelines for ensuring they act in a way that is beneficial to society and individuals. We will discuss the role of governments, organizations, and individuals in shaping these regulatory structures, and how they can promote accountability, transparency, and fairness in AI systems.

Ethical Considerations

Generative AI, like any powerful tool, comes with its own set of ethical considerations. Its potential for good is enormous, but so are the risks if it is used irresponsibly. It is like a well of untapped potential, glittering at the bottom of a dangerous cliff. The challenge is to tackle this potential without falling into the hole of unintended consequences. To navigate this, we must consider ethics.

Ethics, at its core, is about understanding and distinguishing right from wrong. It involves exploring our values and applying them to our actions. When it comes to generative AI, ethical considerations come into play on multiple levels.

First, there is the issue of fairness. As AI systems become more integrated into our lives, making decisions that affect us in tangible ways, the question arises: are these decisions fair? Consider a generative AI used for recruitment. It filters through thousands of resumes, generating shortlists. But what if the AI, learning from past data, starts favoring candidates from certain universities, thereby unintentionally discriminating against equally competent candidates from lesser-known institutions? This is just one example of how an AI can unintentionally propagate bias.

Next, we have privacy. With generative AI's ability to create incredibly realistic content, it's now possible to generate images or videos of people doing or saying things they never did. This raises serious concerns about privacy and consent. Where do we draw the line between AI-powered creativity and invasion of privacy?

Lastly, there is the matter of control. As generative AI gets increasingly sophisticated, it becomes capable of tasks that were once exclusively performed by humans. This leads to a crucial question: Who holds the reins? Who is responsible when an

AI-created piece of content violates norms or laws?

These questions don't have easy answers. They require us to reassess and redefine our ethical frameworks in the light of AI advancements. As we plunge into this complex network of ethical considerations, one thing becomes clear: we need guidelines, a set of rules to ensure the responsible use of generative AI. This is where regulation comes into play. As we transition into this next section, we will explore how we might create a regulatory framework to guide us safely through the generative AI landscape.

Regulatory Measures

To venture safely into the landscape of generative AI, we need more than just ethical considerations. We need regulatory measures—rules that provide a framework for what can and cannot be done, a defined pathway to navigate the danger-ous territories surrounding the well of untapped potential. Regulatory measures act as guardrails, helping us control the power of generative AI without losing ourselves in the abyss of unintended consequences.

However, regulation is not as simple as creating a rulebook and mandating everyone follow it. It's a balancing act, a careful negotiation between encouraging innovation and preventing harm. Too little regulation, and we risk the unchecked growth of AI applications that might pose threats to privacy, security, and equality. Too much regulation, on the other hand, can suppress creativity and hinder progress.

Imagine a startup developing a generative AI system for personalized education, intending to revolutionize how we learn. However, stringent regulations could hinder their ability to collect or use the necessary data, slowing down or even halting their progress. The challenge, then, is to devise regulations that protect individuals and society without restricting the innovative potential of AI.

Regulations must also be adaptable, as AI is a constantly evolving field. Regulatory measures effective today might become obsolete tomorrow as AI advances. For example, early regulations around data privacy might not have accounted for AI's ability to infer sensitive information from seemingly innocuous data—a capability that has emerged only in recent years.

To address this, we may need to adopt a principle-based regulatory approach, focusing on the broad impacts and risks of AI, rather than specific technologies or techniques. This would make regulations both comprehensive and flexible, able to adapt as AI evolves.

International collaboration is another key aspect of AI regulation. Given the global reach of digital technologies, a patchwork of national regulations could lead to confusion and inconsistency. Instead, a harmonized international framework could ensure a consistent approach to AI governance worldwide.

But even the best regulations can only do so much. While they set the boundaries of what's permissible, it's ultimately up to us—the developers and users of AI—to operate within those boundaries responsibly. As we transition into the next section, we will explore this idea further, exploring what it means to use AI responsibly and how we might adopt a culture of responsibility in AI development and use.

Responsible AI Use

Entering the vast field of responsible AI use feels a bit like stepping into a bustling city for the first time. As much as it dazzles with possibilities, it also overwhelms with its complexities. Yet it's these complexities we must navigate to ensure generative AI benefits all of society while minimizing harm.

At its core, responsible AI use involves acknowledging the immense power of generative AI and using it with caution. This means striving for fairness, accountability, transparency, and robustness in all AI applications, from the seemingly routine-like personalized advertisements to the life-changing healthcare diagnostics.

Think of a simple generative AI system used to recommend movies on a streaming platform. Used responsibly, this system could lead to hours of enjoyable viewing, suggesting movies that align with your interests. However, irresponsible use of the same system might result in filter bubbles, where the AI only suggests movies similar to those you've watched before, narrowing your exposure to diverse content.

Similarly, consider a generative AI application in healthcare that analyzes patient data to aid in diagnosing diseases. If used responsibly, such a tool could greatly enhance medical decision-making, leading to timely and accurate diagnoses. But irresponsible use, such as neglecting to test the system on diverse patient data properly, could lead to biased and potentially harmful diagnostic outcomes.

Responsible AI use also means considering the long-term implications of our decisions. For instance, if we train a generative AI model on data that reflects existing societal biases, the AI could inadvertently perpetuate these biases, amplifying societal inequality. Therefore, we need to ensure our data is representative and unbiased, and we also need to regularly audit our AI systems for fairness and accuracy.

While the duty of responsible AI use primarily falls on the developers and deployers of AI, it extends to users and even policymakers. Users must be aware of how AI impacts them, and policymakers must establish guidelines promoting responsible AI use. The responsibility is shared because the implications of AI reach far and wide, touching every corner of our society. Understanding how to use AI responsibly might seem tough, but it's really an important thing to learn.

As we conclude the chapter on ethics and regulation, it is clear how important these ideas are in the big picture of how AI affects society. Next, we will look at how generative AI plays a role in privacy and security. Even before we start the discussion, we can already understand the significance of this topic. As we explore these topics, we will be peeling back the layers, like an onion, to better understand the integral role of AI in our modern digital world.

12

Generative AI - Privacy and Security

I magine leaving your house unlocked every day, or sharing your personal diary with everyone you meet. It sounds unnerving, doesn't it? Now, consider the digital equivalent: your data, your online persona being accessible to anyone with a strong enough algorithm. Welcome to the brave new world of generative AI and its impacts on privacy and security.

In this chapter, we will be navigating through the complex web of how generative AI is transforming our understanding and experience of data privacy and security. As we navigate through the pathways of this complex arena, we will shed light on the opportunities, challenges, and vital countermeasures necessary to ensure a safe and beneficial environment for all.

Impact on Data Privacy

In our digital world, data is often compared to oil, a valuable resource that powers our modern economy. But unlike oil, data is about us—about our behaviors, preferences, and interactions.

When we start talking about generative AI, which thrives on vast amounts of data, the spotlight inevitably falls on the issue of privacy.

Generative AI uses patterns and inferences from existing data to create new data, which sounds simple. But when the data in question is about individuals—their shopping habits, their web searches, even their medical histories—things become a little more complicated. The big question is, who has the right to use this information, and for what purposes?

Let us take targeted advertising as an example. Suppose a generative AI has been trained on your online shopping habits and can predict what you are likely to buy next. This ability can be quite convenient, offering you personalized ads that align with your needs and wants. But on the flip side, how did the AI know you were interested in these items? Who gave it the right to monitor your online behavior? These are the questions that privacy concerns revolve around.

The truth is, in the hands of the wrong people or without the proper safeguards, the power of generative AI could easily be misused, infringing on individuals' privacy rights. Imagine a generative AI system trained to imitate people's writing styles based on their public posts. It could be used to create false statements, impersonate individuals, or even perpetrate fraud, all while breaching their privacy.

Data privacy, though, is not a standalone issue. It is closely tied to a broader concern in our increasingly digital world: cybersecurity. As we venture further, we will dive into the risks and threats posed by generative AI in this domain. As we move on from the world of privacy to that of security, remember, every step we take uncovers new insights, challenges, and opportunities.

CyberSecurity Risks

Let's continue our exploration by focusing on the complex issue of cybersecurity risks associated with generative AI. Imagine, for a moment, walking down a city street. You know the possibility of theft exists, but with secure locks on your doors, a keen eye on your surroundings, and local law enforcement, you feel secure. Cybersecurity, in many ways, works on similar principles. It's about creating that sense of safety, but in the digital world. Now, let us introduce generative AI into this urban landscape and see how it changes the dynamics.

One of the most impactful ways generative AI could intensify cybersecurity risks is through the creation of sophisticated cyberthreats. For instance, generative AI can craft phishing emails so convincingly real that even the most observant among us could fall for them. It could learn from data on successful phishing attempts and generate messages that mimic the style and tone of legitimate emails, making it incredibly difficult to differentiate between genuine and malicious communications.

Moreover, generative AI could play a significant role in propagating deepfakes - digitally manipulated media that portrays people saying or doing things they never did. These are not your average video edits. With generative AI, deepfakes could be practically indistinguishable from real footage. Imagine a scenario where a deepfake video of a CEO declaring bankruptcy is released, causing a company's stock to plummet. Or worse, a deepfake of a world leader declaring war. Such instances highlight how cybersecurity isn't just about safeguarding data; it's about defending the truth and maintaining peace.

Even more, as generative AI systems become more advanced, they could potentially breach even the most secure firewalls, exploit vulnerabilities faster than human hackers, and conceal their activities in ways that are difficult to detect. The higher efficiency and speed of AI systems could drastically increase the potential damage, turning what used to be minor security breaches into catastrophic events.

With these risks on the horizon, it may feel like the digital world is under constant threat. However, while the risks are real and substantial, we are not defenseless. As we explore further, we will discover that the same technology posing these challenges also offers innovative countermeasures and best practices to protect our digital world. As we walk through this digital landscape, we will find that for every looming threat, there is a corresponding shield, a lock for every key, and a solution for every problem. Let us move along to explore the countermeasures and best practices that hold the potential to secure our world against these cybersecurity threats.

Countermeasures and Best Practices

Welcome to the world of digital defense! As we have learned, generative AI introduces unique cybersecurity threats. However, like a true protagonist in a gripping novel, it also presents solutions - the countermeasures and best practices - to combat these risks.

Imagine that you are in charge of protecting your digital world. There are threats coming your way, but you also have various tools and strategies to use. These threats represent the cybersecurity risks, and the tools that generative AI gives us to fight against these threats.

First, let us talk about AI-powered threat detection systems. These systems, fueled by generative AI, can predict potential threats and react faster than any human ever could. They are like vigilant sentinels, tirelessly guarding the castle gates and sounding the alarm at the first sign of an invader. They can learn from previous attacks, adapt to changing tactics, and even anticipate new threats.

Then there are automated response systems, which swing into action the moment a breach is detected. Think of these as the rapid-response force, ready to repel intruders. By isolating affected systems, blocking suspicious traffic, and even launching counterattacks, they can prevent small breaches from becoming catastrophic.

But defending against these threats is not just about reactive measures. We also need preventative strategies—the digital equivalent of reinforcing the castle walls. This is where AI-powered risk assessment comes into play. By analyzing historical data and current trends, these tools can identify weak points in your cybersecurity defenses and recommend improvements, ensuring your walls are always sturdy and secure.

Last, but definitely not least, are AI-driven user behavior analytics tools. These tools monitor and analyze user behavior to identify suspicious activity. They can identify potential threats and suspicious behaviors before such activities can do any harm.

Of course, none of these countermeasures would be effective without human oversight. While AI can provide the tools, humans must provide the wisdom to use them effectively. Regular audits, ethical guidelines, and a commitment to continuous learning are essential. Think of this as the king's wise council, providing guidance and ensuring the castle's defenses are always in top shape.

In conclusion, as we navigate through the web of potential AI threats, it is crucial to remember that generative AI also provides measures to prevent them. It offers both challenges and solutions—risks and rewards. As we look ahead, we can take relief in the knowledge that, with responsible use, we can control the power of generative AI to defend our digital world.

Now that we have explored how generative AI impacts our privacy, security, and ways of working, it is time to set our sights on other impacts of AI.

In the next chapter, we will shift our focus from the topic of privacy and security to a completely different arena, one that may not seem immediately connected with AI but holds crucial significance in our AI-driven future—our environment.

13

The Environmental Equation of AI

A s our digital footprint deepens, there is an unseen footprint that emerges, one that is cast not on the silicon landscape of technology, but on our physical environment.

In this chapter, we will understand the environmental implications of AI, a topic often overlooked in the spotlight of AI's capabilities. Here, we delve into the often unseen but significant impact of AI on our environment and how it can be a powerful tool for environmental sustainability.

Understanding the Environmental Impact

Let's dive into a topic often masked by the shimmering glow of AI's incredible capabilities - its environmental impact. While we marvel at the exceptional feats AI has achieved and continues to strive towards, it's equally crucial to understand the impact it causes on our environment. AI, like any tool, has a cost. Beyond dollars, this cost encompasses the energy required to train complex AI models and maintain the data centers that keep them running.

Have you ever considered the environmental implications of asking your virtual assistant for the weather, or the electricity consumed when Netflix suggests your next binge-worthy series? These seemingly inconsequential actions are the result of complex AI algorithms which require vast computing resources.

Let us visualize it with a study from the University of Massachusetts, Amherst. The researchers found that training a single large AI model can produce as much carbon as five cars would over their lifetimes. Picture five cars, the embodiment of environmental pollution for many, and realize that one AI model's training can equal their combined emissions.

Training AI, particularly large machine learning models, involves a significant amount of number crunching. These computations demand a substantial amount of electrical power, subsequently leading to substantial carbon emissions. The bigger the model, the greater the energy requirement, and therefore, the larger the carbon footprint.

Data centers that house these AI models are enormous energy consumers. According to the International Energy Agency, data centers worldwide consumed about 200 terawatt-hours of electricity in 2019, roughly 1% of all global electricity use. To put it into perspective, that's more than the annual energy consumption of some countries!

Additionally, cooling these centers to prevent overheating also adds to the energy expenditure. The irony here is, the same AI which helps optimize energy usage in various sectors can itself be a massive energy sink.

However, it's not all doom and gloom. Understanding the problem is the first step towards a solution. While the environmental impact of AI is significant, it's not an inevitable consequence etched in stone. Tech giants and startups alike have started realizing the need for "green AI". With energy-efficient algorithms, improved data center designs, and increased reliance on renewable energy, we can look forward to a future where AI's environmental footprint is drastically reduced.

In our journey with AI, acknowledging this duality – its benefits and costs, its achievements and concerns – is integral. As we strive to unleash the power of AI to better our lives, we must not ignore its impact on our environment. Equipped with this newfound understanding of AI's environmental impact, let's shift our focus from the challenge to the solutions, as we explore how AI can contribute to environmental sustainability.

AI and Environmental Sustainability

While the previous segment may have painted a somewhat daunting picture of AI's environmental impact, let's not forget that AI, as a technology, is a tool. Like a coin, it has two sides. We have already seen the costs, the challenges, and the shadows. Now, let us turn the coin over and reveal the other side—hope, solutions, and the potential of AI to combat environmental issues.

Imagine a world where AI helps in accurate climate predictions, improves the energy efficiency of our cities, and contributes to protecting endangered species. This is not a piece of science fiction or a snippet from an unrealistic novel. It's a reality we are gradually edging towards, where AI assists in environmental sustainability.

How does AI weave into the fight against climate change? To tackle a problem, we first need to understand it, and AI shines in its ability to make sense of vast and complex data sets. With climate change being a problem of global proportions, AI has become an invaluable tool in understanding and addressing this crisis.

Consider the world of climate modeling, where scientists try to predict how the Earth's climate will change over time. Climate models are complex and require intense computational resources to simulate various aspects of the Earth's climate system, including the atmosphere, oceans, land surface, and ice. Here, AI can simplify these computations, reducing the time taken to generate predictions and aiding in more accurate climate forecasts.

But AI's potential extends beyond understanding the problem; it offers a hand in solving it as well. For example, AI is increasingly being used to optimize energy consumption. From managing energy grids to reducing energy waste in homes and commercial buildings, AI helps us be more efficient, less wasteful, and thus, more environmentally friendly.

Even in agriculture, AI steps in to provide innovative solutions. It enables precision farming – a practice where farmers utilize AI to understand their crops at a micro-scale, predict their yields, and manage their resources efficiently. This not only reduces the waste of resources such as water and fertilizer but also minimizes the negative environmental impacts associated with traditional farming practices.

AI is also extending its hand to wildlife conservation. By using AI algorithms to analyze images and footage from wildlife cameras, scientists can track and study endangered species more effectively. This, in turn, helps in making more informed conservation strategies.

Based on our discussion, it is evident that while AI's training and running may contribute to environmental challenges, AI applications can potentially provide solutions to some of our most pressing environmental issues. Now, with this understanding of how AI can contribute to environmental sustainability, let us talk about a less-explored territory: the trade-offs between AI's environmental footprint and its potential for positive change.

Balancing the Trade-offs

As we stand on the threshold between AI's environmental impact and its potential to support sustainability efforts, the question arises of how we can strike the balance. How do we reap the benefits of this revolutionary technology without compromising the health of our planet? These are not merely rhetorical questions, but pressing matters that must be addressed as we tread further into the AI era.

On the one hand, we have energy-intensive AI models that leave a considerable carbon footprint. On the other hand, we have AI's incredible potential to combat climate change and promote environmental sustainability. These contrasting elements define AI's environmental equation.

In balancing this trade-off, the first step is awareness and understanding. Recognizing that training large-scale AI models can have a significant environmental impact is the starting point. This knowledge encourages researchers, developers, and organizations to seek more energy-efficient ways to design and train these models. For instance, innovating more efficient hardware, optimizing algorithms, or exploring techniques like transfer learning, which allows a pre-trained model to be used as the starting point for another task, can save both time and energy.

At the same time, it's crucial not to overlook AI's potential as an environmental ally. The same technology that poses a threat can also be part of the solution. AI's role in optimizing energy use, improving waste management, assisting in climate modeling, and contributing to wildlife conservation signifies its power as an agent of positive change. Therefore, actively investing in and encouraging these applications of AI can significantly tilt the balance in favor of environmental sustainability.

Moreover, regulatory measures and green policies can also play a crucial role in this balancing act. Governments and international bodies can encourage sustainable practices in

AI research and application, promoting a shift towards 'green AI'. These measures can include things like providing incentives for using renewable energy sources in data centers or implementing standards for reporting the carbon emissions of AI systems.

We have explored the world of AI from various angles, understanding its impact on healthcare, entertainment, and even the environment. Along this journey, we can understand that AI, in all its complexity, is neither a villain nor a hero. It's a tool, a technology that, like fire, can warm our homes or burn them down. The choice of how we use and control it is ours.

With a greater understanding of the complexities of AI's environmental equation, we now move to a more personal perspective. As AI becomes increasingly part of our daily lives, how will it impact you as an individual? In the next chapter, we explore "Generative AI and You: A Personal Perspective," giving you a perspective into the future where AI becomes a part of your everyday life.

14

Generative AI and You: A Personal Perspective

I magine yourself comfortably settled with your favorite drink, deeply immersed in an e-book that your AI-powered app suggested. It is amazing to think about how smoothly artificial intelligence has blended into your day-to-day routine. From smart homes to personalized playlists, AI is no longer just a topic of sci-fi novels, it is a reality. And this reality is closer and more personal than you might think.

In this chapter, we will take a step back and examine the influence of AI on your life. We will examine how it changed your work, your hobbies, and your interactions. We will then discuss the skills that will equip you for a future created by AI. Lastly, we take a deep look at your role as an individual in shaping this AI-driven society.

Personal Impact

As you switch off your morning alarm, an algorithm wakes up

to your presence. As you start your day, it helps you navigate your actions, whether it is suggesting the quickest route to your office, suggesting a perfect music playlist to accompany your morning jog, or reminding you of an important meeting at work. This is not a futuristic scenario; it is the reality we are living in today, steeped in the magic of artificial intelligence.

Artificial Intelligence has already made quiet inroads into our lives, becoming an invisible companion in our daily chores. Let us consider Alexa, the friendly virtual assistant from Amazon, as an example of AI in action in our homes. She helps manage tasks, plays music, provides real-time information, tells a joke, or even orders a pizza for you. Have you ever wondered how she anticipates your requests, learns your routine, and provides recommendations? This is AI in action, learning and evolving with each interaction to make your life a lot easier.

Our smart homes, driven by AI, can sense and learn our patterns. Lights dim as we sit down to watch a movie, thermostats adjust to our preferred temperatures, and refrigerators inform us when we are low on milk. This seemingly effortless comfort is the manifestation of AI's impact on our personal spaces.

Consider your social media feeds. AI algorithms curate a world tailored to your preferences, based on your behavior, likes, shares, and searches. They introduce you to new music bands, suggest books you might like, show movies similar to those you've watched, and connect you with people with similar interests. All these are examples of AI making your digital space more intimate and personalized.

And then, there's the professional arena. From data analysis to predictive modeling, AI has revamped traditional workflows. It has automated routine tasks, freeing up human resources for more creative and complex problems. For example, AI-driven chatbots handle customer inquiries, allowing customer service representatives to focus on more challenging issues.

Whether you acknowledge it or not, AI has created a profound impact on your personal and professional life. It is no longer just about tech-savvy individuals or businesses. It has become a part of our collective lifestyle, transforming how we live, work, and communicate.

Moving deeper into the era of AI requires us to adapt. We will need specific skills to manage and thrive in this AI-integrated environment. Just as a sailor adjusts his sails to the changing winds, so must we adjust our skill sets to the evolving AI landscape. This brings us to the important discussion of what skills we need to cultivate for an AI-driven future.

Skills for an AI Future

As the prominence of AI continues to surge, a pivotal question arises: what skills are required to navigate and excel in this growing landscape? It is not just about technical skills, though they are undeniably important. It is about cultivating a combination of skills that will empower you to succeed in an AI-driven world.

Data literacy is one such indispensable skill. As AI feeds on data, understanding the basics of data analysis, knowing how to interpret data, and using it to make informed decisions, is crucial. Whether you are a marketer analyzing consumer trends, a writer interpreting reader analytics, or a teacher evaluating student performance, data literacy can offer insightful revelations.

Next, comes problem-solving and critical thinking, skills that are uniquely human and yet crucial for working with AI. As AI takes over routine tasks, the human workforce is left to tackle more complex, abstract problems. Proficiency in critical thinking allows one to formulate and evaluate solutions to these problems, guiding the application of AI to maximize its benefits.

Understanding AI and machine learning fundamentals is another essential skill. You don't necessarily have to be an AI developer, but having a basic understanding of how AI works can be invaluable. It allows you to understand its possibilities and limitations and use it more effectively. Think of it as learning the mechanics of a car. You don't need to be a mechanic to drive, but knowing the basics can enhance your driving experience and even help you troubleshoot basic issues.

Communication skills also remain significant in an AI-embedded world. The ability to express ideas and understand others is crucial in every field, and even more so when dealing with AI. As we move toward AI-human collaborations, being able to articulate goals, tasks, and feedback clearly is essential for harmonious interactions.

Finally, emotional intelligence is a skill that gains prominence in the age of AI. In a world where machines can analyze data and produce results, the human ability to understand, express, and manage emotions becomes a unique asset. In fields such as healthcare, counseling, or customer service, the human touch—the ability to empathize, comfort, or inspire—is irreplaceable.

But even as you equip yourself with these skills, there is something larger at play. It is about the role you choose to play in AI society, the decisions you make, and the ethics you uphold. While AI may be the game-changer, the game itself is played by us, the humans. As we navigate the AI landscape, we must understand our role in shaping this society, and how we can make this AI-driven world more inclusive, fair, and beneficial for all. These questions form the core of the next section.

Your Role in the AI Society

The world of AI may seem complex and vague, like a distant sci-fi reality. However, the truth is that we play a crucial role in this AI-driven society. Your choices, your interactions with AI systems, and your ethical stances all contribute to shaping the AI-infused world we live in and will continue to mold in the future.

Let us begin with an everyday choice: your online behavior. Each time you click, like, share, or comment on the internet, you feed data into the AI algorithms. These algorithms learn from this data, shaping the content you and others see. You are basically part of the ongoing training of the AI systems. Conscious online behavior, understanding the nature of your digital footprint, and considering the impact of your online interactions on these learning algorithms can contribute to creating a more transparent and ethical digital world.

Your use of AI-powered products and services, such as voice-activated virtual assistants or AI-driven navigation apps, also significantly shapes AI society. These choices drive market trends, encouraging companies to innovate and invest in AI technology, thus encouraging its proliferation.

Moreover, as an individual, you are a crucial part of the AI ethics conversation. You have a voice in defining acceptable behavior for AI. For instance, consider facial recognition technology. While it can be handy, raising security and convenience, it also poses concerns about privacy and misuse. Engaging in discussions about such implications, voicing concerns, or advocating for regulatory policies, can contribute to the formation of a more ethically sound AI landscape.

Lastly, your role in AI society is also about preparation and education. The AI future is approaching at a rapid pace, and it is not just about technical jobs or the software industry. AI's reach extends to every sector, from agriculture and healthcare to the arts and education. Embracing lifelong learning, staying informed about AI advancements, and understanding how they impact your life and work can equip you to thrive in this dynamic environment.

As mentioned before, your role in AI society is not merely that of a passive user or observer. You are an active participant, a shaper of trends, a voice in the ethics discussion, and a lifelong learner adapting to AI advances. Recognizing this active role and embracing it is a powerful step toward shaping a fair, ethical, and human-centered AI society.

Our next chapter takes us on an exploration of what's to come—the fascinating future of generative AI. The future may not be crystal clear, but it holds promises and possibilities that are certain to leave you on the edge of your seat!

15

The Future of Generative AI

L et us imagine that we are in the year 2040, and a world-famous musician is releasing their newest album. But this musician is an AI, trained in generations of music and capable of creating compositions that stir the soul, all without a human hand guiding the notes. This may not be an impossible one considering the power of Generative AI.

In this final chapter, we will explore a speculative journey into the future, where the boundaries of generative AI may lead us. We will delve into expert predictions, grapple with the unpredictable nature of technological advancements, and imagine how to prepare for the upcoming AI revolution.

Predicting the Unpredictable

The road toward the future of generative AI is similar to driving on a misty morning; the road ahead is obscured by the unpredictability of scientific discoveries. Today, the world of generative AI is teetering on the brink of spectacular advancements, with each day revealing more of its burgeoning potential.

Consider the possibility of AI-trained scientists making break-throughs at speeds that were previously unimaginable. Their 'minds' may operate 24/7, never fatiguing, endlessly learning, and experimenting. The technologies they invent might revolu-tionize every aspect of our lives, from healthcare and education to art and entertainment.

On the artistic front, we have already seen early forays with AI in writing novels, painting masterpieces, and composing sym-phonies. In the future, we might see generative AI becoming a commonplace tool for artists, musicians, and writers. An AI could conceivably learn your favorite author's writing style and generate a new novel just for you!

One of the most fascinating aspects of generative AI lies in its potential to exceed the limitations of human creativity and problem-solving. Today, our AI models learn from data produced by humans, inheriting our perspectives, biases, and limitations. However, future generative AI might learn from a wider, more diverse range of sources, including other AI models, leading to a creative explosion that could far surpass human capabilities.

Nevertheless, predicting the future of such a fast-paced field is loaded with challenges. Expert opinions may diverge, and even the most educated guess could turn out to be wide of the mark. Many of today's cutting-edge technologies, such as GPT-3 and GPT-4, were barely imaginable a decade ago. Hence, while we can speculate, we must remember that the future may hold surprises that defy our wildest predictions.

While this unpredictability might be intimidating, it is also exciting. It represents a frontier of human knowledge, an opportunity to invent, explore, and understand. This excitement of exploring the unknown, of stepping into a world where AI has matured beyond our current understanding, is part of the attraction of the field of generative AI.

But as we stand in the face of this brave new world, it becomes critical to equip ourselves with the necessary tools and knowledge. The wave of the AI revolution is fast approaching, and we must be prepared when it arrives. We stand at the threshold of an era, much like a surfer awaiting the next wave, poised to dive into the thrilling yet unknown depths of the AI revolution.

Preparing for the AI Revolution

In the heart of a storm, there is a place of calm. And like a storm, the AI revolution can feel overwhelming, fierce, and unpredictable. But with the right mindset and preparations, we can find calm in this digital storm and make the most of the opportunities it presents.

Preparation for the AI revolution is a multifaceted challenge. First, we need to educate ourselves about AI technologies, their uses, and their implications. Not all of us need to become AI developers, but a basic understanding of the technology and its potential is very important. Understanding AI is not a task for scientists alone anymore. It is everyone's business. From students to seniors, every individual stands to gain from having a basic understanding of AI.

Just like literacy was critical in the industrial revolution, 'AI literacy' will be crucial in the AI revolution. It is about understanding how to interact with AI, how to use it responsibly, and how to benefit from it while minimizing the risks. AI literacy also involves comprehending how AI impacts our lives - from the news we read, and the products we buy, to the music we listen to. For example, every time you use your phone's voice assistant, such as Siri or Google Assistant, you are interacting with an AI model that has been trained on massive amounts of data.

The second aspect of preparation is adapting our skills to a changing job market. As AI automates routine tasks, the job market is likely to value creativity, emotional intelligence, and problem-solving skills more than ever. Preparing for this shift may involve re-skilling or up-skilling, but also encouraging younger generations to develop these competencies. Imagine a world where a school's core curriculum includes not just subjects like math and language, but also classes on emotional intelligence, problem-solving, and creativity!

Preparing for the AI revolution also means shaping the ethical and legal frameworks to guide AI's deployment. These guidelines should ensure that the benefits of AI are widespread and its potential harm minimized. Policymakers, researchers, and the public must engage in thoughtful dialogues about privacy, fairness, and accountability in AI.

Finally, mental preparation is as important as the practical aspects. Embracing the AI revolution involves openness to change, curiosity about new technology, and resilience in the face of disruption. Like a surfer embracing the thrill of the wave, we must be ready to ride the ups and downs of the AI revolution.

As we equip ourselves for this upcoming era, we begin to see the outline of a dream. A dream not just of advanced AI systems, but of a world where AI amplifies human potential, empowers us to solve daunting problems, and enhances the quality of life for all. It is this dream, both inspiring and profound, that guides our journey toward the future.

The AI Dream

If the AI revolution is a wave, then the AI dream is the surfboard that lets us ride this wave. It's not about succumbing to the stream of change but about controlling it, guiding it, and turning it into something magical.

The AI dream is not just about machines but also about people. It is a dream of empowerment, of using AI to enhance our creativity, broaden our knowledge, and enrich our lives. It is about using generative AI not to replace human effort, but to amplify it.

Imagine an architect using AI to explore thousands of building designs in seconds, sparking fresh ideas for a sustainable and aesthetically pleasing structure. Or a musician collaborating with an AI to compose unique symphonies, pushing the boundaries of creativity. Or a scientist leveraging AI to analyze complex data sets, speeding up the discovery of new medicines. That is the AI dream. To be honest, evidence suggests that some of these are already taking shape in the world today.

But the AI dream extends beyond individuals. It is about building a society that uses AI to foster equity, sustainability, and well-being. It is about creating smart cities that leverage AI to optimize resources, reduce waste, and improve citizens' quality of life. It is about leveraging AI in agriculture to forecast weather patterns, optimize irrigation, and increase crop yield, contributing to food security. It is about using AI to provide personalized education, ensuring every learner gets the right support at the right time.

However, the AI dream is not a guarantee. It's a possibility, and its realization depends on the choices we make today. It requires nurturing an AI-literate society, fostering a culture of innovation, and shaping ethical guidelines and policies. It involves celebrating the triumphs of AI while acknowledging its challenges, being dazzled by its potential, yet remaining alert to its risks.

As we conclude this exploration of the future of generative AI, we do so with a sense of anticipation and excitement, much like standing on the edge of a thrilling journey. But this journey is not a solitary one. It is a collective work, one that involves all of us – policymakers, educators, technologists, and citizens. It is an adventure of shared learning, imagination, and discovery.

As we step into this future, we do so with the humility of learners, the curiosity of explorers, and the audacity of dreamers. Armed with the insights collected from our journey so far, let us now reflect on the broader implications of generative AI and revisit the questions we have pondered, the insights we have gained, and the dreams we have dared to dream. As we transition to our concluding thoughts, let us remember that every end is but the beginning of a new chapter, the dawn of new possibilities, the birth of new dreams...

16

Conclusion

We had a great adventure exploring the exciting world of generative artificial intelligence (AI). We have moved from understanding the basic idea behind AI to dreaming about all the incredible things it can do. We learned about how AI works, where it came from, and how it became so important today, changing our lives now and promising even more in the future.

We learned about AI's different forms, including the innovative and fascinating field of generative AI. This section highlighted the nuts and bolts of machine learning models and delved into the art and science of crafting algorithms capable of creating new data—from visual masterpieces to stirring poetry and beyond. We grappled with neural networks, understanding how these mathematical models mimic the human brain's function, and exploring how these models, when layered deeply, create extraordinary Deep Learning systems.

One of the essential topics in this journey was the understanding of AI's applications. We discussed the innovative solutions that AI brings to numerous fields, from healthcare, where it aids diagnosis and drug discovery, to entertainment, where it can create new music or even complete a symphony left unfinished. Generative AI is not just a tool for creation; it's a partner in innovation, driving us to horizons we have only begun to imagine.

The role of ethics, regulations, and responsible AI usage played a central part in our discussion. In the world touched by AI, where the line between the creator and the created blurs, we understand the criticality of establishing ethical guidelines and frameworks. Privacy, security, and the paramount need to build AI for good resonated as non-negotiable prerequisites in our exploration.

In the end, we ventured into the world of the unknown, speculating about the future of generative AI. How it might transform societies and industries was not just a theoretical discourse but a necessary preparation for the impending AI revolution. The dream of AI, the quest for artificial general intelligence, was unveiled as the ultimate frontier, the pinnacle of our AI aspirations.

As we close this book, remember that this is not the end but the beginning of your journey in AI. The purpose of this guide is to provide you with knowledge, a comprehensive understanding of generative AI that you can use as a springboard for your exploration. The knowledge you have gained is like a map, guiding you through the diverse and evolving landscape of AI.

The real magic of generative AI comes from using it, not just knowing about it. You have learned a lot about AI by reading this book, and now it's time to profoundly apply that knowledge. Think about how you can use AI in your job. You could be the person who introduces generative AI to your field by bringing the innovation of generative AI to address old problems with new solutions.

Remember, the only constant in the field of AI is change. The landscape of AI continues to evolve, bringing forth new technologies and possibilities. We need to continue to learn, explore, and, most importantly, innovate.

We recognize that the journey of AI leaves an environmental footprint we cannot overlook. However, it's reassuring to know that the same technology, when harnessed responsibly, can also contribute innovative solutions to our pressing environmental challenges, effectively becoming a part of the equation for a sustainable future.

And finally, use this powerful tool responsibly. Ensure your actions align with the ethical guidelines we have discussed. AI is incredibly powerful, but like many powerful things, it can be good or bad. Our responsibility is to make sure we use it to help people and society make the world a better place.

Remember, AI is more than just machines learning and adapting; it is also about us learning to adapt to this AI revolution. So, let us continue to learn, evolve, and shape the future together.

Glossary

Key AI Terms

Below are some of the key terms you will encounter in the fascinating world of AI. We did discuss most of these terms throughout the book. As you get deeper into the subject, you will likely encounter more specific and complex terms. But don't worry—with a solid understanding of these basics, you will be well-equipped to understand and explore the vast landscape of AI!

Artificial Intelligence (AI): AI is the science of making machines do things that would require intelligence if done by humans. This includes problem-solving, recognizing patterns, understanding natural language, and making decisions.

Machine Learning (ML): A subset of AI, Machine Learning involves the design and development of algorithms that allow computers to learn from and make decisions based on data. It's like teaching an old dog new tricks, but with the dog being a computer.

Deep Learning: This is a type of Machine Learning that

mimics the workings of the human brain in processing data for use in decision-making. It's based on neural networks with several layers (hence 'deep'), and it's behind a lot of the exciting AI advancements we are seeing today.

Neural Network: Inspired by our understanding of the biology of our brains—how they learn from experience and recognize patterns—a neural network takes in inputs (in the case of AI, these are typically numbers), processes them in hidden layers using weights that are adjusted during training, and then outputs a prediction.

Generative AI: This branch of AI focuses on systems that create new content, such as images, text, or music, that is similar to human-generated content. It's like an AI artist, but instead of painting or composing music, it generates data that can be just as unique and creative.

Natural Language Processing (NLP): This is a branch of AI that focuses on the interaction between humans and computers using natural language. The goal of NLP is to read, decipher, understand, and make sense of human language in a valuable way.

Supervised Learning: This is a type of Machine Learning where the AI is trained using labeled data, that is, data paired with the correct answer. Like a student studying with a textbook that has the answers at the end, the model learns from this data to make accurate predictions.

Unsupervised Learning: Unlike supervised learning, unsupervised learning involves training an AI using no labels at all. The AI just looks for patterns in the data. It's like learning to play a sport by just playing the game, instead of doing drills or practicing specific skills.

Reinforcement Learning: This is a type of Machine Learning where an agent learns to behave in an environment, by performing actions and seeing the results. For example, while training a dog - good behavior is rewarded and bad behavior is penalized, and over time, the dog learns to behave in the desired manner. Similarly, AI learns from previous results and learns to behave and adapt accordingly.

Robotic Process Automation (RPA): This technology allows anyone today to configure computer software, or a "robot," to emulate and integrate the actions of a human interacting within digital systems to execute a business process.

Popular Generative AI models

Below are a few of the most popular and widely used generative AI models out there. As you know, the field of generative AI is evolving rapidly, and new models are being developed all the time.

Generative Adversarial Networks (GANs): A type of generative AI model that comprises two parts: a generator, which produces fake data, and a discriminator, which evaluates the data. The generator tries to fool the discriminator, and in doing so, it learns to create increasingly convincing synthetic data. GANs are often used to generate realistic images, audio, and text.

Variational Autoencoders (VAEs): VAEs are another popular generative model. They encode input data into a lower-dimensional latent space and then decode it to reconstruct the input. The generative aspect comes into play during decoding, where the model can generate new data by decoding random values in the latent space.

Transformer Models: Transformer models are a type of model used in natural language processing. They use attention mechanisms to weigh the importance of different words in a sentence. Some of the most popular transformer models include the GPT-3 and BERT.

GPT-3 (Generative Pretrained Transformer 3): Developed by OpenAI, GPT-3 is a transformer model known for its large scale and impressive capabilities in generating human-like text. It has 175 billion parameters and has been trained on a wide variety of internet text and code, and can generate creative, coherent, and contextually relevant sentences.

GPT-4 (Generative Pre-trained Transformer 4): Developed by OpenAI, GPT-4 is a transformer model that is even larger and more powerful than GPT-3. It has been trained on a dataset of text and code that is 100 times larger than the dataset used to train GPT-3. GPT-4 has been speculated to use around 100 trillion parameters, which gives it the ability to generate even more creative and informative text than GPT-3.

BERT (Bidirectional Encoder Representations from Transformers): BERT is another transformer model developed by Google. It is unique for its bidirectional training, which allows it to understand the context of a word based on all of its surroundings (left and right of the word).

CycleGAN: CycleGAN is a type of GAN used for image-to-image translation tasks, like turning a horse into a zebra or a painting into a photograph, without needing paired examples.

DCGAN (Deep Convolutional GAN): This is a type of GAN that uses convolutional layers in its generator and discriminator networks, making it more suited for image tasks.

StyleGAN (Style Generative Adversarial Network): This is another type of GAN, developed by Nvidia, that's especially good at generating highly realistic images. It is most famous for the site "This Person Does Not Exist," which generates images of non-existent people.

Seq2Seq (Sequence-to-Sequence) Models: These models are used for tasks that involve sequential data, like language translation or speech recognition. They use an encoder to compress the input sequence into a vector, and a decoder to generate the output sequence.

AI websites

As we discussed in the book, AI is being used in all sorts of ways today, from helping doctors diagnose diseases to recommending what movie you should watch next. The websites we will look at will show you just how much AI is changing our world. They are all about the different ways AI can solve problems and make things easier or better. Remember, these are just a handful of websites to give you an idea. There are several websites being built every single day that use AI technology to enhance the work people do every day.

ChatGPT - AI Chatbot Website

ChatGPT is definitely the hottest AI website that broke the internet in 2023. Developed by Open AI, it is a web-based conversational AI chatbot. ChatGPT utilizes state-of-the-art language processing AI models and was trained using vast amounts of information—articles, books, web texts, Wikipedia, and other pieces of writing on the internet. It is capable of understanding and processing natural languages. You can ask questions, and ChatGPT will generate human-like responses to your queries.

Midjourney - AI Image Generation Website

Midjourney is one of the most popular and powerful artificial intelligence websites for image creation. It lets you generate stunning digital art and images from plain text. Just enter text to describe what you want, and Midjourney will produce a series of images based on your text prompts. You can use it to generate backgrounds, realistic photographs, paintings, 3D illustrations, logos, and a whole lot more.

Jasper - AI Writing Website

Jasper is an AI website that helps you write a variety of copy and content quickly and effortlessly. From blog articles and social media posts to website content and marketing copy. In addition, it supports creative writing tasks, such as poetry, stories, and lyrics.

Synthesia - AI Video Creation Website

Powered by artificial intelligence, Synthesia can easily convert any piece of text into a high-quality, compelling video in just a matter of minutes. Moreover, Synthesia enables you to create interactive and engaging videos with virtual human-like presenters. You can choose from a library of AI-generated presenters or create an AI presenter of yourself with your own voice.

Beautiful.AI - AI Presentation Maker Website

Beautiful.AI changes the way you make presentations. All you need to do is input your text, and Beautiful.AI will generate stunning presentations for you automatically. Using Beautiful.AI can save you a lot of time and effort since you don't have to edit presentations manually. Beautiful.AI also offers smart AI features like automatic layout design, smart resizing, content suggestions, and even data analytics.

Notion - AI Productivity Website

Notion is a powerful cloud-based productivity tool where you can take notes, create to-dos, tasks, and schedules, manage projects, and more. What makes Notion apart is its AI-powered features. It uses artificial intelligence to assist you in summarizing notes, improving writing, translating content, brainstorming ideas, and more. Notion represents the next generation of cloud notes.

Soundraw - AI Music Generation Website

Soundraw is an online AI music composition tool that allows you to create original and customizable music easily and quickly. Simply choose the mood, the genre, and the length of the music you want, and Soundraw will automatically generate songs according to your specifications! You don't need any musical skills or knowledge to use Soundraw. It's designed for everyone, from beginners to professional musicians who need high-quality music fast.

Avatar. AI - AI Website for Creating Avatars for Social Media

Avatar.AI uses cutting-edge AI technology to change your photos in cool and creative ways that are sure to impress. Just upload your photo, and you'll get high-quality, realistic AI avatars that look just like you but in various styles and scenarios. You can transform yourself, your friends, or even your pet into desert punk warriors, a zombie at Halloween, an Instagram model, the main character in a video game, or a fashion model.

Let's Enhance - AI Image Enhancement Website

Let's Enhance can improve the quality of your photos, making them sharper and clearer in an instant with just one click. Let's Enhance also enables you to upscale photos to a higher resolution without quality loss. It's perfect for photographers, designers, and anyone else who needs high-quality images for their work.

DeepArt.io - Artwork creation

DeepArt.io is an AI-powered website that allows designers to generate unique and stunning artwork. Once you upload an image, the website's AI algorithms will transform it into a piece of art in a matter of seconds. Deepart.io supports various styles, including impressionism, cubism, and futurism, making it a great tool for designers looking to add a touch of creativity to their work.